D0378890

RAISE

—THE—

BAR

Creative Strategies to Take Your
Business & Personal Life to the Next Level

By
Mike Vance and Diane Deacon

CAREER PRESS
Franklin Lakes, NJ

Copyright © 1999 by Intellectual Equities, Inc.

RAISE THE BAR

Cover design by Tom Phon
Printed in the U.S.A. by Book-mart Press

To order this title, please call toll-free 1-800-CAREER-1 (NJ and Canada: 201-848-0310) to order using VISA or MasterCard, or for further information on books from Career Press.

The Career Press, Inc., 3 Tice Road, PO Box 687, Franklin Lakes, NJ 07417

Library of Congress Cataloging-in-Publication Data

Vance, Mike.
   Raise the bar : creative strategies to take your business to the next level / by Mike Vance and Diane Deacon.
     p.   cm.
   Includes index.
   ISBN 1-56414-392-9 (hardcover)
   1. Creative ability in business. 2. Organizational change.
3. Success in business.   I. Deacon, Diane, 1960-   . II. Title.
HD53.V353   1999
   658—dc21   99-22504
                                               CIP

Dedication

This book is dedicated to those people who
raise the bar *and make the world a better place.*

Acknowledgments

Val Halamandaris, Peg Cushman, Steve Steffke, Dennis Walch, Don Costantino, Steve Jobs, Warren Turski, Eric Salama, Mike Jenkins, Jack Welch, Frank Ponzio, Scott Johnson, Gary Wendt, Ken Dobler, Tom Pickett, Scott Woods, Arlyn Rayfield, Tom Yonker, Michael Eisner, Ricki Fairly Brown, Don Spear, Richard Morrison, Jim and Ellie Newton, Tom Guest, Joe Rolero, Steve Kaufman, Dr. John Noseworthy, Dr. Hugh Smith, Dr. Natarajan, George Fink, Dr. Dave Savello, Scott Evanoff, Hon. Max Cleland, Mark Vance, Mike Gustafson, E. Cardon Walker, Dave Abdo, Larry Broedow, Danny Cox, Peter McNally, Bruce McCaw, Manny Martinez, Larry and Shirley Deacon, Karl Litzinger, Sandy Sphatt, Ken Kurt, and Sandy Cameron.

❑ CONTENTS

Walt Disney took his seat at the front of the conference room on the third floor at Disney Studios to hear preliminary ideas for the entrance of a new entertainment complex that eventually would be known as Walt Disney World in Orlando, Florida. Little did those of us on the team who attended that briefing know that, within a few weeks, Walt would be dead of lung cancer. The world would weep at the loss of a creative genius who was without equal. His final exciting project would be left to others to complete, but it was destined to become one of the world's premier resort destinations, setting the bar higher for everyone else.

Mike Vance had been working on the entrance complex project for several months. He remembers that eventful day for several reasons. Walt usually rushed quickly into a room, but on this day he was deep in thought and was noticeably preoccupied. As the meeting began, he was anxious to get going. An immense issue was on his mind: How to make the new project better than anything they Disney had ever done before.

Mike knew something special was going to happen: He knew that Walt was warming up to the prospect of creating something very big—the Florida project.

A meeting with Walt often took the form of a briefing. Each was truly a one-of-a-kind event. (A briefing is a short and to the point status update on a project, allowing others to give input and voice any concerns.) To this day Mike clearly remembers the feeling of deep respect that ran through his mind as he watched the great impresario conduct this briefing. Often, he would add provocative comments that shed an entirely new light on the issues the team members had been struggling with for days. Walt could summarize an issue succinctly in a way no one else had thought to do. The process of creative thinking energized him and everyone else.

After an idea was presented from the team on the entrance complex, Walt chimed in with his thoughts, adding an innovative twist that made the solution better. He did this time after time, getting better, sharper ideas as the discussion went on. After only a few exchanges, Walt was radiating an energy and vitality that everyone else in the room could feel. There was none of the restlessness or boredom that mark customary meetings most of us attend. Instead, there was the passion, commitment, and brilliance that only a fine leader can help create. His eyes sparkled, even though he was tired from a full day's work. Mike made a mental note to himself to remember that, on this late afternoon, how effective Walt was at stimulating creative spirit in others. "If only we all could learn to stimulate others like Walt did," Mike thought to himself. Walt had taken this special team, a team with people who were being prepared for leadership roles for the Florida project, and used penetrating questions and observations to inspire them to raise their work and thought process to a whole new level. In just a few moments, and with a few questions and observations, Walt raised the bar for everyone in the room...including himself.

Mike left the briefing knowing that he'd learned some unique techniques from Walt on how to stimulate creativity and standards higher.

Getting hooked on raising the bar

After Walt's untimely death, Mike knew that what he'd learned in that briefing was a clear example of what made Walt (and the organization he built) superior. In virtually everything he did, Walt Disney found a way to move himself and his organization up to the "next level." He found a way to get people to focus on new challenges, commit themselves to new goals, and examine long-standing problems with fresh eyes. If there were any single characteristic that reflected Walt Disney's way of doing business, it was his passion for raising the bar.

Walt didn't like sequels. He didn't like doing things the same old way. He didn't like solving this year's problems with last year's solutions. He wasn't satisfied with resting on his laurels.

When we discuss raising the bar, we're not simply talking about getting people (or ourselves) excited or about instituting short-term positive change. We're talking about what Disney accomplished on so many projects and for so many years in his organization—the habit of raising the level of performance in such a dramatic, exciting, and powerful way that no one ever wants to go back to the old ways of doing things.

Raising the bar takes what is currently being done and makes it better. It enhances the quality and uniqueness through innovation and creativity. The standards in which things are done are elevated to a higher level, which people then come to expect.

Raising the bar means getting committed to new, better, more energizing ways of doing things. It means committing yourself to a regimen of higher performance and goal-enhanced achievement. The idea of going back to the "old way" isn't just unappealing—it's unthinkable! After all, we don't want to create a brand new "same old thing." The process of raising the bar will give others the feeling they're sharing in the fundamental creative processes that animate the universe.

Stir things up! Rattle some cages! Slaughter the sacred cows! Break away from the crowd! We are talking about implementing a unique way of thinking, a way that enhances one's being and heightens an organization's existence. These were the hallmarks of Walt's inimitable style.

Dinner with the dreamer

After that strategy briefing, Walt took the team members to dinner and shared with them dozens of his ideas about setting ever-higher standards as part of an everyday process. Mike was so impressed with the ideas Walt shared that night that he made a point of writing them down on paper afterwards. He was glad he did! Here are some ideas on making personal and organizational improvements that Walt passed along during the dinner conversation with his team:

1. "The most important lesson I've learned is to avoid making sequels and repeating last year's success."
2. "The big secret is to keep reaching out, moving ahead, blazing new trails, challenging yourself, and rising above difficult situations by getting a new perspective, a new point of view..."
3. "Try not to address this year's problems with last year's solutions."
4. "When we develop a project, we examine it from every angle. We explore every possibility."

Walt put principles such as these into action, which raised the bar in his own business. Consider his momentous decision to launch Disneyland, an entirely new kind of amusement concept called a "theme park." To do this, he had to raise the standards for himself, his organization, and an entire industry! In committing himself to this goal, Walt took the amusement park business, which had previously had a reputation for shoddiness, lax business practices, and general moral turpitude, and completely transformed it. He did this by "walking around the problem from every angle" and developing a creative plan that would allow his company to do a more effective job than anyone else in that industry was doing at the time.

This process was in keeping with Walt Disney's overall business philosophy. He was committed to doing tasks better than anyone else did them, and he was not interested in people who wanted to rest on their past achievements.

A group of college students once asked Walt how they could become rich. He handed them a business phone book, told them to open it to any page, place a finger down at random on a listing, and whatever that business was doing, make it better than it had ever been done before. This story is repeated often in the Disney organization...and is what motivated the company to build Disneyland in the first place!

On Saturdays, Walt often took his two daughters, Sharon and Diane to Griffith Park in Los Angeles for a day of play. This is a large park that was very popular among children; it featured a miniature train ride, a pony ride, an old collection of trains, and a huge carousel set high on a hill overlooking the park.

One particular Saturday, Walt walked up the hill and placed his girls on the carousel for a long ride. He sat on a nearby bench, watching them ride the wooden horses. As he sat, he held their popcorn and cotton candy. The popcorn, he noticed, was stale. The cotton candy was limp.

According to Disney lore, he thought to himself at this point: "There is nothing worse than limp cotton candy." The employees who ran the carousel looked and acted dumb and had the personality of bored security guards.

He then noticed the horses on the carousel. Every horse on the ride was meant to be a jumper going up and down, but only the outside row of horses were actually going up and down. There is probably nothing worse than being a little girl and getting on a carousel horse that won't go up or down. To make matters worse, the paint on many of the horses was chipped and peeling.

All of these flaws bothered Walt. They caused him to pick up a pencil and sketch out early ideas he had on a sketchpad that he carried with him. Those ideas were the beginning of what would eventually become Disneyland.

Walt once said, "I wanted to create a place where a daddy could go and have as much fun as his little girls and boys were having. Just imagine if you're a little girl, looking forward all week to taking a trip to the park with your daddy, and you get on a horse that won't jump. Add to this chipped paint, stale popcorn, limp cotton candy, and unpleasant employees—what a disappointment!"

To raise the bar, Walt's standards were the seminal ideas for a metaphor we developed at Disney University: "A place where all the horses jump and there's no chipped paint." The carousel became a symbol of the mission that resulted in Disneyland, the mission that took the amusement park business to a new level, one that incorporated ideas no one had ever heard of before. The "theme park" was born.

The foot draggers say the following:

➤ "If it ain't broke, don't fix it."
➤ "Don't make waves."
➤ "We do a good enough job."

These excuses are used to avoid accepting the challenge of continuous improvement. They will cause the bar to go lower and failure will replace success sooner or later. They are anti-progress. They make us lazy!

You don't need to be sick to get better! You don't have to have flat sales in order to do something to grow the business. You don't need to have a catastrophe in order to move your business to the next level.

The saying is trite but true: Water that stands still becomes stagnant and polluted, because closed systems die. Organizations and individuals that don't commit themselves to raising the bar lose ground to the competition and will eventually die.

So ask yourself and others "What's new and improved?"

We have to keep growing and keep creating the "new-and-improved." This book contains eight basic strategies to help you and your organization be better than the best by lifting standards to set new records and continue to win challenges we undertake.

Famed hockey player Bobby Orr was constantly asked how he got to be such a legendary player. Once, a reporter actually told him he was "perfect" on the ice. Orr's response was illuminating: "Nothing makes you perfect. Practice only makes you better."

This book will help you practice by utilizing unique tools and techniques, while implementing a process that will help you become a champion. The process requires patience, commitment, and practice.

Walt Disney once responded to critics that he was a perfectionist by saying: "I have the one quality necessary to be a true perfectionist. I'm usually patient. You can never achieve the lofty dreams you have if you're a perfectionist who's impatient."

Not everyone is patient enough to follow through on the goals that really matter. We hope the strategies we offer help you raise the bar continually, just as Walt committed himself to excellence and incorporated it into a culture that lives on. This is a way to become "better than the best" in your chosen field.

RAISE THE BAR CHART

ACHIEVE GOAL		
Strategy 8	Keep the Creative Spirit Alive and Growing	*Raising the bar higher*
Strategy 7	Roll Out and Implement	*Prepare closures, deliverables, and launch plans.*
Strategy 6	Communicate and Organize	*Transfer knowledge, information, and resources.*
Strategy 5	Breaking Out of the Box Into the Creative Zone	*Train for revival of the fittest.*
Strategy 4	Develop People to Become Pathfinders	*Utilize ideation techniques.*
Strategy 3	Create a Detailed Master Plan	*Develop the MICORBS strategy.*
Strategy 2	Think Out of the Box: Master the Art of Innovation	*Adopt the formula for success:* $$\frac{F + P^1}{V + M} = C^1$$
Strategy 1	Build a Strong Foundation	*Ask the nine fundamental questions.*
LAUNCH		

Go for the gold!

❑ INTRODUCTION:
Becoming Better Than the Best by Raising the Bar

Jack Welch, chairman of General Electric, was participating in a lively briefing on a light bulb project with his GE team at our creative thinking workshop. As usual, Jack was leading a highly charged discussion. He makes a habit of challenging people's thinking—yet at the same time he inspires their imaginations. The results are usually remarkable.

At one point, Wayne Heilman, the Halarc project manager, asked Jack, "You want us to make sure that what we do is the best—isn't that right, Jack?"

His response was worth putting in a picture frame. "Absolutely not!" Jack responded, "The best isn't good enough. We want to be better than the best!"

In that instant, Jack laid down a motivating challenge to *raise the bar* of performance by setting higher standards. Too often, what passes for the best in a given situation is, in reality, quite mediocre. We should withhold our personal judgments on what is or isn't "the best" until the bar is actually raised through improvement and innovation.

The inherent challenge of raising the bar should be analyzed in its current social context. The American Dream could be slipping away as more and more individuals continue drifting into a two class society: the haves and the have nots, the knowledge worker and the muscle worker, the rich and the poor. It behooves us to keep the promise of the American Dream alive and well—and one great way to do this is to promote what we call electronic literacy.

Literacy is the ability to read and write. Electronic literacy is the ability to use the computer and other technology. A stroll through the burgeoning populations of our inner cities is often sad and disheartening. A lack of knowledge has disenfranchised millions of our citizens. The gap widens as peoples' psychological well-being, self-esteem, and self-worth are diminished because they can't read and write well. Gaps in literacy and electronic literacy are now both major issues for our society, and we won't be able to resolve them unless we commit ourselves to raising the bar. The current "best" just isn't good enough.

The biggest, most central, issue taken up in this book is Jack Welch's challenge to be "better than the best." It challenges us to make our standards higher and our expectations more grandiose. We are becoming too average.

Raising the bar, step by step

This book is divided into eight strategies for raising the bar in your business and personal life:

Strategy #1: Build a strong foundation

A strong foundation is built by asking and analyzing fundamental questions. This establishes a baseline on which to raise the bar and measure results. A solid foundation is built on developing core competencies and correcting any existing faults. It's learning to face the facts and fix the cracks.

Strategy #2: Think out of the box

As Charlie Brown put it, "You can't think new math with an old math mind." Learn to get out of old thought patterns into new and innovative thinking habits. Discover where your Creative Muscles are and how to stimulate and exercise them! Through this strategy, you adopt a unique thinking formula for success that has been producing effective solutions.

Strategy #3: Create a detailed master plan

Avoid being in the planning phase while you are executing ideas. Many organizations lack a method to capture good ideas, as well as develop and detail their thinking for creating a plan of action. Learn how to use our effective MICORBS process. This methodology will help you develop a vision, as well as a detailed plan, for combining strategies to raise the bar to new heights.

Strategy #4: Develop People to Become Pathfinders

You can't grow beyond your good people. There is nothing that compares with a blueprint for developing talented and competent people. Then continue to develop them to the next level. The emphasis with nearly every outstanding leader is to start with good people. Mike Vance's expertise, as former Dean of Disney University and head of idea and people development programs, is captured in this strategy. Learn how to identify and develop Pathfinders—then let them set you where you want to go. These training techniques can also be used to bring about a "revival of the fittest," awakening people who have talent and ability to contribute at peak levels.

Strategy #5: Achieve Break Out of the Box Solutions

Good ideas are not accidents. Smart thinking just doesn't happen. Solutions are only temporary events. You need a process to keep innovative breakthroughs coming. Solutions are achieved when we utilize a variety of effective techniques and methods, instead of brainstorming. These concepts, tools, and techniques come from years of applications from companies that relentlessly increased their performance. In this strategy, you learn how to break through "sacred cow" barriers while maintaining the "cash cow" flow.

Strategy #6: Communicate and organize

What happens to good ideas? Often, nothing happens at all. Many worthwhile ideas get lost because they are not effectively communicated and organized for implementation. Learn exceptional techniques to transfer knowledge, information, and resources for achieving your goals.

Strategy #7: Roll out and implementation

Be on time and under budget. Many people carry the ball, but can't score, often because they don't have a detailed, roll-out plan. Implementation is often one of the weakest areas in personal and business planning. Too many ideas fail at the implementation phase. In this strategy, you'll learn how to overcome that problem.

Strategy #8: Keep the creative spirit alive and growing

Here you will learn how to create a culture of continued creativity and innovation to raise the bar higher through pathfinders, heroes, champions, and role models. You will see how the creative spirit can excite and exhilarate.

Disney's "secret"

Walt Disney was often asked by a group of college students how they could become rich like him. Walt added to his response, "The way to get rich is to do what you do better than it's ever been done by laying out your strategies."

These strategies will allow you to raise the bar to reach new heights by building a strong foundation using think out of the box concepts and strategic master plan creation that will lead to breakthrough solutions while you develop people to be models and champions.

Walt Disney, who often said "We're only as good as our next picture," was never one to rest on his laurels or relish his past achievements. He lived in the present with one eye on the future. He knew the Creative Muscle must be constantly flexed or it would atrophy from lack of use. Living to maintain the status quo did not interest him in any way, although he had a profound respect for history. He was a consummate innovator who understood that one's credentials were never permanent, but had to be continually earned by creative achievement.

He exercised his Creative Muscle by always reaching out, pushing ahead to the next project and challenging his people to do the same, to raise the bar above their last accomplishment.

The entrepreneurial race

Walt's life is a poignant reminder to us that it's time to step up and raise the bar by starting our creative engines again. There's a hot new race in town called the "Entrepreneurial Revolution." It's one of the fastest races ever run in history. Nearly everyone is trying out for the qualifying rounds in what we call the Entreprenuerial 500. Whether we're an entrepreneur or an intraprenuer (working within a company) we owe it to ourselves to find out what the competition is doing out there and how to keep up with them.

The entrepreneurial race is running on a entirely new type of raceway. In fact, this race is becoming an entrepreneurial revolution that is changing the way we live and work. The brand new track is under permanent construction, adding considerably to the degree of difficulty and complexity of the race. This innovative raceway is being run on the Information Superhighway. As we make our way onto this road, we definitely need a valid driver's license. We must understand how to race in order to win.

The new driver's license is called "Entrepreneurial Thinking," but there's no age requirement for it, and the only road test for qualifying for a license is technological knowledge and spirit. We've discovered some hot race tips from experienced drivers we have known that will help you to win the big prize. These tips work equally well when applied to business or personal life found in these eight strategies.

We have to become a nation of doers, and of risk takers again, with a foundation of renewed constructive values. In order to compete, in order to really win, we need more than just productivity and quality. We must change our way of living, freeing ideas and originality that only come from entrepreneurial thinking, taking us beyond solving this year's problems with last year's solutions. Sequel after sequel, in cars, movies, and sitcoms are boring us to death. The tyranny of "sameness" and "repetition" are perniciously encasing our spirits.

Today, far too many of us are playing it safe by relying on corporate consultants and support groups to run our lives and businesses. We need to do our thinking. We need to learn the grace of taking the blame instead of looking for some other person to take it. We need to succeed on our own.

The road to the top is for people with entrepreneurial thinking in their fuel tanks. It's for people who have got to be in the race, no matter what—whether they're running alone, overseeing others, or contributing to attaining the goals of the organization for which they work. You can spot them anywhere because their engines are revving and they are ready to go. They can't wait to get started—they're ramped up and ready to go right now! They want their foot off the breaks and onto the accelerators. They are generally bold and aggressive.

We will demonstrate how to apply key strategies for creative, continuous improvement in entrepreneurial thinking to your workplace and your career through the analysis of proven concepts of how to raise the bar. We will offer actual case histories and examples of the challenges and the opportunities we're likely to face. We'll explain how every career demands improved strategic thinking on a continuous basis. We'll discuss the skills, the actions, the attitudes, and the steps we must take to think like an entrepreneur. But, more essential to success is having qualities that can be admired by others because of adherence to morality and decency.

There are many businesspeople and entrepreneurs out there who don't complete the race, because they fail to commit themselves to creative thinking and habits of continuous improvement. Their lives and businesses often flounder hopelessly. It seems that they move forward two steps and then back four steps. We want to uncover the principles that will raise the bar, and keep raising it, until devotion to perpetual excellence is a reality in our careers and in our personal lives. The challenge is we are looking for high-octane fuel for our engines, because we can't run on empty for very long in this competitive race!

We're either in the race or "out of it." This is a race that never ends. When we cross the finish line, we have to refuel and start over again. The strategies we'll be studying in *Raise the Bar* need to be applied continuously to keep your creative juices flowing.

Entrepreneurial strategies for raising the bar

Start a program to raise the bar right now within your company or in your personal lives, on either a small or a large scale. There are eight strategies and each one is the subject of a chapter. We can use these strategies to stimulate our thinking and we can pass them along to team members or anyone we wish to motivate toward entrepreneurial thinking by raising the bar to the next step. The entrepreneurial spirit is demonstrated in the following story:

The coconut pickers, sorters, and counters

Six frightened people suddenly find themselves shipwrecked on a desert island in the middle of the Pacific Ocean. It's a small island with only 10 coconut trees, each heavily laden with large coconuts. They land on the island around three in the afternoon. At five o'clock the same afternoon, one of the six says, "We've got to get these coconuts off these trees and organize them into equal piles by sundown!" The other survivors are a little suspicious of this idea. Why should they bother categorizing coconuts now? There are more important matters—there's going to be a beautiful sunset to watch in a few hours on the beach. What's the hurry? But the first castaway insists, and soon all six are busy plucking coconuts from the trees and organizing them into piles. The more piles, and the more types of coconuts, the better!

That first castaway, the one agitating the others to organize the food supply, is, of course, the dedicated entrepreneur. The entrepreneurial spirit will make itself known anywhere, and we know that means everywhere. Even out in the middle of the Pacific Ocean, with no other signs of authority or civilization in sight, and with a beautiful sunset beguiling them to look. If there are trees with coconuts, there's going to be one person who wants to make sure they're off the trees and on the ground to be used for some purpose.

Another event occurs when the entrepreneur gets the ball rolling—there's the accountant in the group who says, "Can I count the coconuts? I'd love to figure out exactly how many coconuts are in each pile."

There's another person who lives just for the fun of picking the coconuts from the trees, rather than counting them. That's the vice president of operations. Once the job starts, these folks love to be in charge of determining exactly how the coconuts are going to be picked, where they will be piled, and what the daily quotas will be.

Someone else in the group desperately wants to be in charge of approving the coconuts. Is the length of the "hair" on the outside of the shell appropriate? Is the size right? Is the color satisfactory? Is this, considering the qualifications, the right coconut for us? This is the human resource person, or the personnel director. These folks enjoy passing judgment on the various coconuts to make certain they meet their standards. He asks, "Are they our kind of coconuts?"

Of course, there's also the person who takes the time to laboriously hide the coconuts on the other side of the island, burying them in places no one would ever think to look. Before the shipwreck, this financial planner, was in charge of establishing tax shelters and estate plans, hiding valuables for the future.

Finally, there's the person who keeps trying to talk people out of picking coconuts in the first place. They corner everyone, one by one, admonishing them by saying, "I just want to bring to your attention the fact that there may be hostile natives on another island nearby. It is rumored they consider these precious coconuts to be sacred objects with religious meanings. The risk is just too high, I recommend that we put this project on hold." That's the lawyer in the group—complete with Rolex watch, wingtip shoes, and a huge bill. However, the groups calculate that they that the nearest island is more than a hundred miles away and says, "We'll risk it."

The six "supporting characters" are interesting, and they always play important roles in starting anything. But the person who provides the motivation to get the initiative going, and passes it on to others, is the entrepreneur. This is the person who:

1. Sees an opportunity and seeks to fulfill it (utilizing the supply of coconuts).
2. Evaluates and accepts the risk (how far away are the natives on the other island?).
3. Organizes people to achieve the task (with stunning speed—people feel they're organizing themselves).
4. Manages people through instructions: "You do this, you do that, and by the time sunset rolls around, we can sit back, look at the piles of neatly arranged coconuts, and say, 'Look what we achieved today! It's time for martinis and pina coladas!'"

These are actions that reflect an underlying entrepreneurial spirit. This is how the future gets built. This is how the bar gets raised. Someone takes the initiative to inspire everyone to do better. Long live the pickers, the counters, and the sorters!

Signs that you need to raise the bar

How can we tell whether our organizations or ourselves need to take advantage of the ideas contained in these 13 strategies— and learn to raise the bar? If you see any of these 13 conditions, it's time to evaluate the need for change! These conditions lead to committing *faults*, just as we do in playing tennis when we step out-of-bounds.

1. No longer a leader in your field.
2. People do the same thing, the same way, for too long.
3. Subtle or no improvement in customer satisfaction.
4. Inability to retain good people.
5. Difficulty in adapting to change.
6. Routine and fixed procedures prevent people from getting much accomplished.
7. Ideas generated are of generally poor quality and unrealistic.
8. People are focusing more on internal politicking than they are on innovative thinking.
9. Ideas are not being put into practice; initiatives may be discussed, but nothing new ever seems to get delivered.
10. Products and/or philosophies are not in sync with the times.
11. Frequent reorganizations and changes in leadership; the guiding philosophy appears to be "When in doubt, reorganize or merge with the natives."
12. Sales and profits are not growing.
13. Improvements only come through various mergers and acquisitions.

Facing the faults

We need to face the faults that we have as a prerequisite before we can raise the bar. Most of us don't want to face the facts about our own faults. People who are ready to raise the bar are willing to acknowledge exactly where they are and what obstacles face them.

Most of the time, the great British leader Winston Churchill knew exactly where he stood, and wasn't afraid to speak frankly about the problems he (and others) faced. On one occasion, Churchill was attending a party, and had had way too much to drink. A matronly lady beheld the condition of the famous Prime Minister of England with considerable distress, walked over to him, and said sarcastically, "You, sir, are drunk!"

Churchill peered over at her and, without missing a beat, said, "Yes, madam, it is true. I am drunk. And you, Madame, are ugly. However, tomorrow morning, I shall be sober." Churchill certainly did face his faults!

❑ STRATEGY #1:
Build a Strong Foundation

"The foundation of a business must be strong, solid, deep-rooted, and flexible for growth"
-Diane Deacon

Roots and cycles

Diane read a fascinating little book by Jerzy Kosinski entitled *Being There* by Jerzy Kozinski, which was sent to us by a Creative Thinking Association member, Roy Vineyard. (In the 70s, the book was made into a popular movie that starred Peter Sellers and Shirley MacLaine.)

The main character, Chauncey Gardener, grows up without a formal education or family. His only two pursuits for many years are gardening and television. However, a series of serendipitous events puts him in the position to offer his opinion regarding the troubled economy to the president of the United States. When asked about the economic conditions at the time, Chauncey says, "I am a gardener. Growth has its seasons. There is spring and summer, but there is also fall and winter, and then spring and summer again. As long as the roots are not severed, all is well and will be well in the garden..." The president is heartened by this observation; he points out that many people lose sight of the fact that nature and society are parts of the same whole.

Chauncey had a point. While we accept the inevitable seasons of nature, we get upset by the natural seasons of our economy and business. In business, there is a time for spring and summer; but unfortunately, as in a garden of the earth, there are also times for the inevitable chill and storms of autumn and winter. These seasonal conditions often crack the foundation. However, as long as the seeds of a business remain firmly embedded in its foundation, growth will flourish again.

In order to weather the seasons, the foundation of a business must be strong, solid and deep-rooted before we can begin to raise the bar again. Even though the roots are deeply embedded, they still need to grow. If the roots are too firmly embedded and inflexible, it's hard to raise the bar. A strong wind could break the tree.

Consider, for example, the beautiful Hotel del Coronado near San Diego, California. This is an old historic resort hotel that has been operating since the days of candlelight. In fact, when the time came, Thomas Edison himself did the electrification of the facility! However, the management has maintained the strong, solid foundation of tradition while raising the bar and incorporating the latest, state of the art amenities, making the Hotel del Coronado one of the finest hotel and convention facilities in the state.

Foundations, baselines, and alignments

The time: the early 1950s. Major General Leo M. Kreber, commander of the Ohio 37th Infantry Division, stood in the dank Louisiana air at midnight waiting to greet his men, who were due to arrive by troop trains. A military band was playing John Phillip Sousa's "Stars and Stripes Forever" as the long train approached the station. He stood at attention, puffing on a cigar, saluting his men. Mike was one of them.

The pomp was muted by the lateness of the hour and the gravity of reporting for active duty during wartime. General Kreber understood how much time, effort, and organizational planning were involved in moving 10 thousand men and equipment over a stretch of thousands of miles. He understood that building a strong foundation, establishing baselines, and ensuring proper alignments were essential for the success of the mission. (D-Day was still relatively fresh in everyone's memory. It represented one of the monumental military operations of history, an armada of unprecedented proportion that has been documented in hundreds of war films.)

The military power structure, one of the oldest of organizational forms, has practices that we can all learn from in building strong foundations. For example, the administration and logistical mobilization of an infantry division for active duty is a herculean task, demonstrating Strategy #1.

The foundation work behind each and every soldier that the general met that night was extensive and complex. Reams of paper work are nothing new to anyone who has served in any branch of our armed services. However, experience has shown that snafus anywhere in the system can cost lives. The standards must be high, because lives are at stake!

The following is a list of 12 individual forms Mike recalls from his military experience that had to be filled out and completed on every soldier in triplicate. These forms were completed during interviews with each person who was going on active duty and required considerable time to complete.

Foundational forms

1. General Information Survey (two pages).
2. Complete Medical History and Physical Exams.
3. Separate Immunization Chart.
4. Financial Deductions/Paycheck Allotments.
5. Clothing and Equipment Issued.
6. Fitness Reports and Promotions.
7. Special Citation and Awards.
8. Weapons Certifications and Training.
9. Qualification Courses and Training.
10. Preparedness Check List.
11. Serial Number, Dog Tags, and IDs.
12. Photographs.

Dates had to be checked and verified by different leaders representing different functions, sections, and specialties. The typing of the forms alone added hundreds of hours to the processing, where time was a critical factor. The hard lines of military organization exacerbated the need for efficiency.

Improving the baselines

A baseline of approximately one year was established as the time required from starting the paperwork on a single soldier to the train arriving at the basic training camp. Baseline schedules and objectives were often delayed because of unforeseen circumstances. This could prove to be disastrous when 10,000 solders were supposed to relieve a tired, battle-weary division on the line. Thus the question arose, how could this baseline be improved?

Someone suggested that it was time to raise the bar: "Let's reduce the administrative preparation by 50 percent."

Baselines are achieved by raising the bar of performance with commitment from realigned functions and leadership. Someone looks at conditions the way they really are, wonders why are they that way, and asks, "How can we improve this?" Alignments now become necessary to meet the higher standards.

Alignments

The 12 foundational forms that had to be completed cut across every part of the infantry rifle company. A change in the procedures for processing these forms would require the cooperation and alignment of everyone concerned.

Colonel Harold L. Hays, Chief of Staff for the 37th Infantry Division, encouraged Mike to work on this challenging problem. The goal was established to raise the bar by reducing the time required for completion by 50 percent. This was not an easy task, but succeeding at it would save precious time and money.

First, one master form was designed that included all the information found on each of the 12 individual forms. This master form wasn't meant to replace the 12 forms...just to keep them from holding up the men!

Second, it was decided to hold only one interview (instead of 12) with each soldier to complete the master form. This would save many hours.

Third, it was decided that it was not efficient to have only one or two typists working on the project. Others were "enlisted" by aligning other organizations in the community to help with the typing. A local high school agreed to provide 50 typists and to complete all of the 12 forms from the master form.

Finally, it was decided to have all the forms that required a signature be executed simultaneously.

The results of this project exceeded even the optimistic goal of 50 percent! The four-step initiative reduced the time spent on paperwork by 70 percent, and raised the bar dramatically at a foundational level.

Mike learned three important creative and administrative principles from this army experience early in his career:

➢ Solid foundations require a review of core competencies that help people establish a "launch point" to raise the bar.

➢ Alignments establish a reduction of redundancies, enhance synergies, and streamline operations and communications.

➢ Baselines give us a reading of where we are at any moment so we can establish measurements of growth and progress. (For example, EKGs or mammograms give your physician a point at which to monitor your health. The cardiologist orders a stress test for a heart patient in order to establish the baseline of blood flow. After a procedure is completed, another test is ordered and compared to the baseline.)

FABs (Foundations, Alignments, and Baselines) are essential to your health...and the health and well-being of your business! Below is a reality checklist to begin the process of figuring out where to raise the bar from.

The Foundational Questionnaire

Foundations

1. What are your core competencies (list)?
2. What are you "better than the best" in (describe)?

3. Are you inflexible in our core competencies (examples)?
4. Are there any emerging technologies that might crack the foundation (name them)?
5. Where are your faults or cracks (test for them)?
6. Which core competencies helped you raise the bar in the past (case histories)?

Alignments

1. Do all of your core competencies (foundation) complement one another and work efficiently together?
2. Which core competencies don't fit and yet help or give you a competitive advantage?
3. Which core competencies don't fit and hurt you by draining your resources?
4. What have been new core competencies, new visions, or other factors that precipitated the need for alignment or realignment (historical perspective)?

The Baseline

1. How do you rate your activities on a scale of 1-10 (10 being the highest)?
2. Are you below the bar in any of our core competencies?
3. What baselines do you compare yourselves to (last year's bar chart, our competitors bar chart, historical data, and so forth)?
4. How do your faults rate to your successes?

On the next four pages are charts that will assist in thinking through your FABs. Take these charts and fill them out to establish your launch points, along with areas where you need to raise the bar. Identify some areas (core competencies and activities) you wish to improve upon. Then, identify what level you wish to raise the bar to.

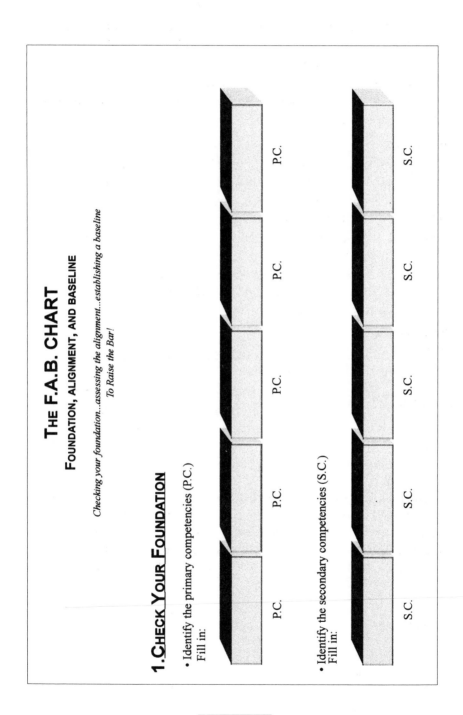

THE F.A.B. CHART
FOUNDATION, ALIGNMENT, AND BASELINE

Checking your foundation...assessing the alignment...establishing a baseline
To Raise the Bar!

1. CHECK YOUR FOUNDATION

• Identify the primary competencies (P.C.)
Fill in:

P.C. | P.C. | P.C. | P.C. | P.C.

• Identify the secondary competencies (S.C.)
Fill in:

S.C. | S.C. | S.C. | S.C. | S.C.

The F.A.B. Chart
Foundation, Alignment, and Baseline

2. Assess the Alignment

• Are they aligned correctly?

• Do they need to be realigned?

Fill in:

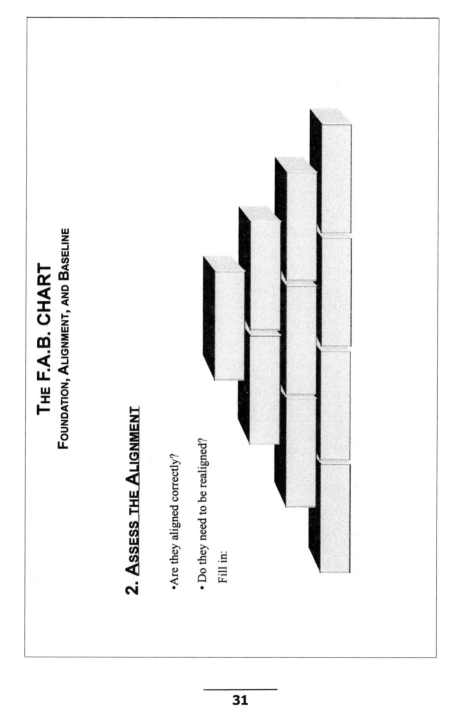

THE F.A.B. CHART
FOUNDATION, ALIGNMENT, AND BASELINE

3. ESTABLISH A BASELINE

Rate your primary competencies and your secondary competencies on a scale of 1-10. (10 being the highest rating)

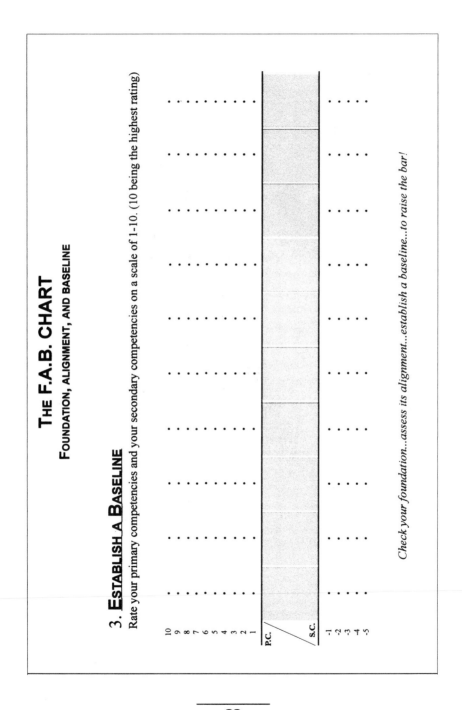

Check your foundation...assess its alignment...establish a baseline...to raise the bar!

The F.A.B. CHART OVERVIEW

FOUNDATION, ALIGNMENT, AND BASELINE

For checking your foundation...assessing the alignment...establishing a baseline To Raise the Bar!

1. CHECK YOUR FOUNDATION

• Identify the primary competencies (P.C.)

• Identify the secondary competencies (S.C.)

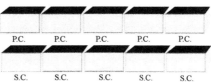

2. ASSESS THE ALIGNMENT

• Are they aligned correctly?

• Do they need to be realigned?

3. ESTABLISH A BASELINE

Rate your primary competencies and your secondary competencies on a scale of 1-10. (10 being the highest rating)

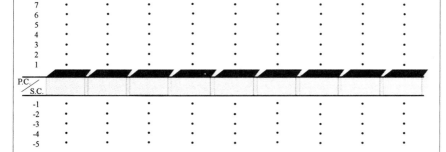

Check your foundation...assess its alignment...establish a baseline...to raise the bar!

What is Your Bar Rating: _____

9 questions to help raise the bar

The following nine fundamental questions to ask and analyze can help build a strong foundation for a raise the bar campaign. One note of caution is necessary: When building or strengthening any foundation, analyzing your baseline, or making alignments, be certain your foundation is not sitting on top of an active fault! Use the following nine "foundational" questions to help ensure that your efforts to raise the bar are on solid ground each step of the way. Take appropriate action to repair any faults before beginning. This establishes a baseline at the start, permitting you to monitor progress. The bar cannot be raised until a strong foundation has been established. Throughout history, emerging technologies have a substantial impact on the existing foundation. Countless old businesses have been made obsolete by technological advances. At the same time, they gave birth to entirely new industries based on these technologies. This causes dramatic upheaval during the transition period that can be weathered with astute thinking and planning.

These nine fundamental questions are intended to be analytical, not critical. These nine questions are:

1. *What* are things really like? (Clearly identify the need.)
2. *Why* are they the way they are? (A cause behind the effect.)
3. *How* will change be implemented? (Concepts and examples.)
4. Is the plan realistic and deliverable? (Logical and valid.)
5. Is everyone genuinely change-oriented? (Open and willing.)
6. Is incompetence sanctioned? (Don't ignore the problems.)
7. Have ideas been formed into a vision? (The goal or objectives, including a method.)
8. Are there people on the team with ability? (Experience, education, and training.)
9. Is everyone prepared to see the project through to the end? (Implementation and action.)

(See our book, *Think Out Of The Box*, pages 141 through 151, for a broader discussion of these nine fundamental questions.)

Question 1: What are conditions really like?

We begin by asking what the situation is at the moment by identifying and uncovering needs or problems that require a solution. This demands realism in analyzing the way conditions are, if we hope to improve them. This question helps us focus on the status quo—what's actually taking place. It's necessary to guard against allowing political, prejudicial, or financial "filters," (our own or those of others) to distort our perception of reality. It's essential to obtain valid, objective information about initiatives we're working on if we hope to correct flaws and make our effort succeed.

Caveat

Obtaining valid information about why conditions are the way they are is rarely an easy task! A tenacious effort by everyone is required. This is the first step in research and development; it calls for the investment of money and time and the surveying of a cross section of people to uncover the truth. An essential requirement for discovering the truth is not to lie or distort your findings. It's common knowledge among experts of creativity, that many leading inventors, composers and artists had a propensity for honesty. They knew that distortion would lead to almost certain failure. Aristotle expressed this idea by saying that "A is A." Something is what it is, not whatever we want it to be. Seeing reality the way it really is, serves as a cornerstone in building a strong foundation to raise the bar of human performance. We can do almost anything in life as long as it is within the realm of truth and within the operating general principles of the universe. It's the denial of these principles that causes so many of the world's serious problems.

Question 2: Why are things the way they are?

When we ask the question "why," it reveals the cause behind the need identified in the answer to question one.

Caveat

Don't let the first explanation of "why" conditions are the way they are stand unchallenged. In many cases, the actual reasons behind the challenges we face are both complex and multifaceted. We can't assume there is only one determining factor in the situation we're analyzing and make the false assumption that the answers needed will be apparent by talking to only one person or evaluating one group of data. This question of why things are the way they are is meant to uncover the cause behind the effect which is revealed in question number one.

Socrates taught his philosophy students the Law of Causality. He taught them to ask questions about observed "effects" in order to ascertain the cause behind them. This is referred to as Socratic Thinking. Leaders often want to improve the performance of their people by using critical rather than analytical thinking. Managers will often criticize, berate, and belittle their people instead of providing them with the tools and resources to actually raise the bar. Negative criticism is a form of short-range thinking that produces no positive, long-term results. In this case, the effect is low performance and the cause behind it (the why) is lack of skills, understanding, and tools. Dr. Maria Montessori called this "the principle of cognitive reasoning," or the ability of being fully aware of the reason behind something. This ability is crucial if you are to raise the bar.

Imponderables

There are circumstances when finding the answer to the question "why" will raise imponderable questions. We are frustrated when confronted with facts that seem incapable of being weighted or evaluated with exactness.

"Who created the universe?" "Is there life after death?" "Is there a heaven and a hell?" The list of imponderable questions can go on forever. There are those who believe these questions are answered by their religious teachings. There are others who believe these questions cannot be answered.

Nevertheless, there are many questions that seem to be imponderables at first glance, but turn out to be explainable and understood after careful thought and research. This is precisely why we must be diligent in laying down foundations for raising the bar.

For example, it was not long ago when nearly everyone suffering from a serious heart attack died. Today, this is no longer true because doctors, scientists, and researchers refused to be discouraged by imponderables—they persisted, and their tenacity created procedures, equipment, and medicines that have saved millions of lives.

As a result, there are heart centers, much like the Heart Center of Sarasota, Florida, founded by Dr. Ponnusway Natarajan and his team of physicians like Dr. Mathew Koshy, who are chasing the imponderables.

Dr. Natarajan, who lives near Mike, visited him one day. During their visit, the doctor was sketching a new device he was thinking about for a heart procedure.

Imponderables can stimulate curiosity and motivate us to raise the bar of civilization to a higher level. Imponderables can cause us to flex our creativity as did Dr. Natarajan. Imponderables can lead to the building blocks of a strong foundation.

Young children can often drive adults crazy with an endless list of "why" questions. Their curiosity can also be dampened by ignoring their questions all together, or by giving them a perfunctory answer.

Question 3: How can we promote change?

The answer to this extremely practical question leads directly to developing a blueprint for helping yourself and others raise the bar.

Caveat

Failing to provide both the concepts *and* the examples of success employed by other people will tend to lower the bar instead of raising it. Exercising theory alone doesn't achieve success. Search for the historical perspective, and find out if what you have in mind has actually worked for someone else in similar circumstances. (The first three questions are called the "core" questions in building foundations.) We need to allow considerable time on these core questions in order to have the best chance of fulfilling our goals. Parents, like leaders in business, have a desire for their children to excel by making high grades in school. The effect is the desired goal of making "As." To do it, one must uncover the cause of lower grades. It will then be easier to provide the tools to get straight As. This is an example of analyzing rather than criticizing behavior if we want to correct a problem.

An example how

The "how to" of accomplishing a goal or objective takes us immediately beyond the theoretical into the practical world of methods of assuring success. As you may know, stimulating children to get good grades is a thorn in the side of many parents.

The wise parent knows that children often don't know how to get exceptional grades because they are rarely taught how to study, take notes, and read for content. It is more important to show children examples of making an academic record that they can be proud of, rather than simply trying to motivate them to study. Providing them with the tools, the skills, and the habits to arrive at the goal changes self-doubt into self-worth.

Question 4: Is our plan realistic and deliverable?

Is what we're contemplating logical and valid—or is it just a cloud of smoke? How much credibility does this plan deserve? We have to rework a plan until we can be as certain as possible.

Caveat

Avoid settling on a plan that is realistic (that is, capable of being carried out under ideal conditions) but not deliverable (capable of being carried out given the time and resources available to you). Walt Disney often used to remark that fantasy is born in reality. He said, "You must first be well grounded in the way things are in order to take off into fantasy, imagination, and dreams." Walt Disney World in Orlando, Florida, stands as an example of what can be done in a swamp if we have a reality-based dream. He called this kind of thinking, "Imagineering."

Question 5: Are we really change-oriented?

This question establishes whether or not the organization and the individuals involved are actually open to the changes a proposed plan entails. Or are we going to create smoke and mirrors and therefore, in the end, change nothing? Alfred E. Newman of *Mad Magazine* said, "Just because everything has changed doesn't mean anything is any different."

For example, we recently flew into the St. Thomas, Virgin Islands airport to facilitate a project development session with one of our clients. We had a 6 a.m. flight from San Juan, Puerto Rico. Diane was trying to find a restaurant or concession stand for a cup of coffee in the newly remodeled airport, but at that time of morning, the only store open was a perfume shop. The plane landed in St. Thomas (another newly remodeled airport) and a set of stairs was rolled up to the plane now parked on the runway (new and improved?). We got off the plane, and walked down the stairs onto the runway. We proceeded to walk and walk and walk around the *outside* of the airport! After a few miles of hiking around the outside of the airport we finally arrived *inside* the airport. Diane asked the security guard, "Why are we not allowed to walk inside the airport?" The security guard's response was that the airport was designed to only have departing passengers inside of it. The people arriving at the airport are to walk outside. This change was made to simply implement change, and not for the sake of improvement! Implementing real change is one of the biggest challenges we face in life and business. Diane then proceeded to the baggage claim area. While waiting for her luggage to arrive she asked another security guard where the ladies restroom was located. She was directed over to the restroom but found it locked. She rushed back over to the security guard to ask why the restroom door was locked. The security guard replied, "Well it's not open today." Diane responded, "Well okay, I'll just wait until tomorrow to go!"

Innovations and breakthroughs are just the beginning. What happens when the time comes to implement the *new* ideas in the plan? Don't change for the sake of change, but be change oriented! Conditions will change—it is inevitable. However, we need to make good on the change promised. A well planned implementation good on the change promised. A well planned implementation strategy is an essential part of the creative process! (See Strategy #7 for a detailed discussion of this issue.)

√ Caveat

Don't expect to buy into a plan that involves radical change if it doesn't incorporate input from the people whose lives it will affect, or from people who will make change happen. Find out what people expect from the changes in your plan and consider giving them a voice in the way those changes will be phased into the organization. Listen to the ideas and concerns people have about the changes in the plan. It's important to understand that change occurs incrementally—it rarely happens instantaneously. Important requirements for accommodating change are overlooked if rewards and recognition are not given to participants who make major contributions.

Question 6: Do we sanction incompetence?

Do we sanction incompetence by ignoring it? We're not talking about the "learning curve," or the initial training period that is necessary to learn new ways of doing tasks. Instead, we're talking about deep-rooted attitudes that reject learning and attempt to maintain the status quo. If it's "too much work" to root out incompetence when it's damaging your organization (for instance, antagonizing your customers), then campaigns to raise the bar will probably not succeed until reality is faced. It's a challenge to take constructive actions about problems. It's often easier just to ignore them, but challenges are what raising the bar thrives upon for achieving improvement.

Caveat

Taking the easy way out by turning a blind eye to incompetence is like not noticing a blinking neon sign. Not long ago, Mike was putting in a wake up call at a hotel for 5:30 a.m. when the front desk clerk asked if he could wake up later. Mike responded, "Why do you want me to wake up later?" The clerk replied, "There are too many people waking up at 5:30 a.m." Mike said to him, "When would you like me to wake up?" The clerk said, "We have an opening at 5:45 a.m." Mike was too tired to argue so agreed to the 5:45 a.m. wake up call. However, the call came at 5:30 a.m., even after the clerk's badgering. It was absolutely the worst hotel that Mike ever stayed in. He had a talk with the hotel manager the next morning, hoping to help prevent it from happening to someone else.

If we don't sanction incompetence, we have to teach people through effective training how not to be incompetent.

Question 7: Are our ideas now our visions?

Vision refers to an organization's long-term goals and our personal long-term goals. This question brings fundamental issues into agreement with the long term objectives we envision. This question also stresses developing methods that will lead to achieving our vision. When our short-term steps lead us toward the ultimate goal we're pursuing, when we know that pursuing this plan will solve the immediate problems and move us closer to the goals we have established—then we're on the right track. We recommend the vision be communicated with a story, so everyone understands it clearly.

Caveat

Avoid implementing a plan that is in direct conflict with the organization's larger goals—or failing to develop long-term goals in the first place! It is essential that deeply held values aren't in conflict with the vision because the cross currents can lead to failure and demotivation of the team.

Create your own Main Street, build a castle of your own

Mike attended an auto industry dinner with a man by the name of Dr. Mortimer Feinberg, Ph.D., the senior industrial psychologist at Ford Motor Company, as well as the author of a unique book entitled *Why Smart People Do Dumb Things*. Mortimer and Mike found themselves sitting next to each other at the dinner. He extended his hand to Mike and said, "Are you Mike Vance?" Mike shook his hand and told him he was, which made a broad grin work its way across Mortimer's face. "Mike," he said, "I've have been looking forward to meeting you ever since I heard you were going to be in attendance here. I've been eager to meet someone who knew and worked with Walt Disney. I've got about a million questions for you. I hope you don't mind!"

Mike assured him that he didn't mind talking about Walt—it was one of his favorite subjects, and an engaging conversation began. For about an hour, Mortimer peppered Mike with questions about what it was like to work with Walt. The first question he asked was by far the most interesting: "If you had to give a eulogy at Walt Disney's funeral, what would you say?"

Mike said, "What a wonderful question. It's one of the best questions I've ever been asked." Mike thought about it for awhile and said, "You know one of the greatest portrait photographers in the world was Yousef Karsh, a man who had taken photographs of statesmen, presidents, and every kind of dignitary imaginable. Karsh took a remarkable photo of Walt. Beneath it, he placed a description that I believe may be the best summation of the man's life. In part, it stated 'Underneath this breezy exterior surface, lies a deadly serious man, who is concerned with only one thing—the laughter of children.' I would show the people at that funeral the photo, read them the description, and tell them that, when I was at Disney, this was always the vision: the laughter of children. That was Walt's mission. That's what made him tick." Mortimer smiled. You could tell he liked the answer.

One of the big reasons people get messed up, one of the reasons smart people do idiotic things, is that they lose sight of their mission, their vision. Sometimes, they forget the vision because it's too hopelessly complicated. They refuse to remember it! Walt Disney was a man who took infinite care, and built an organization of extraordinary complexity around a single simple idea—making children laugh. He never lost sight of that vision. If something didn't make children laugh, or didn't make an adult's inner child laugh, Walt was highly skeptical of it.

Mortimer asked another question: "What motivated Walt at the deepest level?" Mike responded, "I believe there were really two things. The first was his love of children. If you asked him what he was doing it all for, you'd get that answer: happy children. That's why it says 'Welcome to the Happiest Place on Earth' over the entrance to Disneyland. But there was something else that not many people know about Walt. In his childhood days in Kansas City, he was a paper boy who delivered an early morning paper often during the wintertime when the morning temperature could be far below zero. To warm himself, he would find a spot in an apartment hallway and cover himself with layers of newspaper. He used to say that, as he lay there, bundling newspapers around himself, he found himself thinking, 'I've got to do something so that, when I grow up, I won't ever be cold like this again.' And if you pressed Walt for the reason he was successful in life, he'd sometimes smile and say, 'I'm trying to stay warm!'"

These were very simple, very powerful motives. They helped Walt keep in touch with his vision—and to raise the bar again and again throughout his life. We have tried to learn from Walt Disney the purity of simplicity and the power of an uncomplicated vision. Keep your motivation simple, and you won't lose sight of the vision!

Question 8: Do we have able people on the team?

Ability is defined as "the capacity to achieve." When we face this question, what we're really asking is: Do we have the experience necessary to accomplish this task? Do we have the education necessary to implement the technical aspects of this plan? Do we have the combination of talents that will help us identify the problems we're going to face before they become catastrophes? We've worked in organizations where people on some teams simply didn't have the necessary skills to attain their objectives. Also, the excessively bureaucratic culture of corporations and organizations kills people's ability and destroys their incentives to achieve.

Caveat

Be careful when accepting someone's estimation of their own capacity to achieve success rather than an objective evaluation of their skills. If you don't have direct experience with a person's work, you should find out exactly what experience they have from a third party. How close did he or she come to fulfilling the requirements for this project? People often let their enthusiasm and optimism get the better of them when asked to evaluate their own talents.

One company we know with several hundred franchise units in the food industry faced issues of ability realistically. For example, they noticed that new units they were opening constantly failed to pass inspection on quality and standards. The management decided to halt franchising temporarily while they analyzed the cause of this problem.

The cause emerged quickly—a lack of managers with the ability to run their stores. In other words, their capacity to accomplish the task was below standard. In response to their findings, they initiated an intensive management training and leadership development program before resuming franchising activities. This strategy was successful. They resumed opening new stores, and are one of the largest chains in their field. There were other companies with the identical problem who didn't curtail their expansion and met with disastrous results. These companies have since gone out of business.

Question 9: Will we see this implemented?

This question refers to roll out, execution, and action, subjects we'll be discussing in forthcoming strategies. We know that skilled leadership is the catalyst to accomplishing closure and attaining the vision. This question examines whether or not we can rally skilled people, resources, and effective ideas to put into practice.

Caveat

Credentials alone will not ensure final success. All too often, the first questions we ask a new team member are: "Where did you go to school?" or "What degree did you earn?" People with impressive credentials can achieve remarkable success. But those credentials, in and of themselves, were not what made achievement possible. Formal credentials may open up a few doors, but they can't ensure that he or she will be a functioning team member. In evaluating your team (and yourself), place more emphasis on accumulated experience—and a minor emphasis on degrees, certifications, awards, and so forth. Whatever you do, don't assume that, simply because someone has an advanced degree from a prestigious school, he or she has the necessary leadership qualities to execute the plan.

Building Main Street and castles

General Motors asked us to work with one of its technology groups under the leadership of Dennis Walsh. We have worked with Dennis for a number of years and know he likes to get right at the issues, face the facts, and get a vision in place that is achievable. Mike was talking about the design concept at Disneyland in California and the Magic Kingdom in Orlando, Florida, as an appropriate metaphor for building a strong foundation.

There was nothing like seeing Walt walk down Main Street in the park or waving at people when driving one of his antique electric carriages. He loved to walk down Main Street and stop in front of the beautiful Sleeping Beauty's Castle.

Princess Caroline of Monaco once visited Disneyland when she was a little girl and received a personal ride down the street with Walt and the press.

The two of them posed for a picture in front of the castle. Walt asked Caroline with enthusiasm, "How do you like my castle?" She said, "It's a beautiful castle, but it's not as big as mine." That comment made the front pages of newspapers around the world. "Princess Tells Mickey's Dad 'Castle Okay.' " Walt's reaction to this story was simple and direct: "I've got a little girl telling me my castle isn't big enough—by God, we'll build one in Florida that no one can miss!"

Main Street created a gathering place for band concerts, parades, special events and, most important, a place that serves as a visual hub for the various lands of Disneyland. It served to unify the parts by tying them together. The castle was set at the very end of Main Street and was visible from the entrance all the way down the street. Its beauty symbolized the fantasy of Disney and became the logo for the park.

The castle was built first at the Orlando park in order to capture people's imagination, and give them a preview of what was coming. It was almost comical to see this magnificent structure rising up out of an old swamp into Florida's beautiful blue skies. Some of the Florida locals would deride the castle by saying, "Those Hollywood guys from California don't know what they are doing—a castle in a swamp. That Disney is kooky..."

However, as the construction crews began to watch the buildings frame up on Main Street, U.S.A., their comments and opinions changed and the ridicule ceased. One, tobacco chewing local standing at the train station looking down Main Street remarked, "That's a hell of a sight. A castle in a swamp complete with a town, streets, and shops. I'm beginning to get it." This was exactly what Walt wanted them to get. He said, "In any project, always build your castle first. Let it be your vision to inspire others and motivate them to do outstanding work." Visionary castles can help to raise the bar. Main Street became the entrance and connection to each of the other lands: Tomorrowland, Fantasyland, Frontierland, and so forth. Main Street tied everything together, creating a solid foundation.

Walt viewed Main Street as the foundation that made Disneyland work efficiently. It was a nostalgic reminder of yesterday for guests strolling down the street looking through the stores: the Main Street Emporium, the clock shop, the candle maker, a barbershop, even an old fashion grocery with a place to play checkers around a pot belly stove. There was even a wooden Indian at the tobacco shop on Main Street.

Let's use Main Street and the castle as a metaphor to study today's organizational challenges. In business we have been organized primarily into departments, and at home we have various rooms. The boundaries around each of these divisions are fixed and are not flexible. Technology came along, changing the structure for organizing people. Technology acts like a Main Street, cutting across organizations, removing the lines, and creating what we now call a boundary-free culture. Technology ties together the divisions into common pools.

By asking these nine fundamental questions, we establish a strong foundation and baseline to build our own Main Street, serving to unite and tie together the departments, just as it does for Disneyland and Disney World. Main Street for a business can serve as a foundation for core competencies, a starting point to raise the bar. It can also be visualized and developed in a physical place called a Team Center. This brings the parts together with technology and a visual operating process called Displayed Thinking. (A Team Center is a creative environment that provides resources for individuals and teams to promote creativity, innovation, communications, teamwork, and action plans) We will talk more about these effective environments and processes throughout this book.

Our challenge in raising the bar starts with a strong, solid foundation. If this is not the case in your organization, then you must first identify the faults and fix the cracks in your foundation.

Principles for raising the bar: Strategy #1

✓ Check your foundation to make sure it is solid.
✓ Make sure your core competencies and other activities are aligned for efficiencies.
✓ Identify a baseline to establish a launch and measuring progress.
✓ Asking each of the nine fundamental questions with honesty and accuracy.
✓ Follow a series of planned strategies for raising the bar from the beginning. (This book can be used as your checklist.)
✓ Avoid skipping one of the eight strategies presented or glossing over them.
✓ Have a simple, clear vision that you and others can understand and act upon.
✓ Have the passion to push beyond normal endurance to raise the bar.

Personal applications

Personal applications are examples of each strategy used at the personal level.

A foundation of strong values

Mickey was the name Mike Vance was called throughout childhood. John E. Vance was his favorite uncle.

A fresh, wet snow was falling on Christmas Eve in Greenville, Ohio, making the surrounding area as quiet as a giant sound stage. Car tires made a brittle, crunching sound as they passed over snow. It was very cold.

Mickey, who was eight years old, was already in bed waiting for Santa Claus. Suddenly, he heard the doorbell ring and he leaped out of bed and rushed to the window.

As he looked out from his second story window, he saw shadows reflected from the living room fireplace, and dancing across the snow-encrusted sidewalk. He looked down at the sidewalk and strange imprints in the snow outside caught his attention.

He saw a pattern of two small holes, each the size of a quarter, followed by long, deep drag marks in the snow, about three feet in length—they extended from the curb all the way up the walk to the front door.

The curious marks were make by his Uncle John, who walked on crutches because of the crippling effects from his bout with childhood polio. Mickey was excited because he loved his Uncle John very much.

Mickey's mother, Virginia, answered the door. "Hello John, Merry Christmas! What on earth are you doing out in this nasty weather tonight?" she said.

Uncle John said, "Merry Christmas, Virginia. I came by to see if Mickey could help me on my Christmas Eve rounds. He is old enough now and I really need help to get gifts in and out of my car. It would be a great experience for him."

She said, "Well, he's already in bed. I doubt if he's asleep though. Do you still take gifts to the county jail? It would be a memorable experience for him. I'll go get him dressed to go along with you."

After dressing, Mickey got into Uncle John's car for an adventure. The car was equipped to make it possible for a polio victim to drive. Uncle John actually had one of the very first cars equipped with these features. Mickey enjoyed riding in the car because everyone wanted to look at it.

Their first stop was to buy the gifts at the local variety store for the people they would visit on their rounds. Their shopping list consisted of:

➢ Five small Christmas trees.
➢ Five boxes of candy bars.
➢ Five Christmas wreaths.
➢ Five rolls of summer sausage.
➢ Five wind-up phonograph players.
➢ Five records of Christmas music.
➢ 50 miniature Bibles.

Mickey placed these gifts in the back seat and trunk of Uncle John's car. It was always tricky, requiring some ingenuity to make them fit in the cramped space. After the packing was completed, they made their way to visit the following places:

1. The Greenville City Jail.
2. The Federal Prison.
3. The Sinclair Old Folks Home.
4. The County Orphanage for Children.
5. The Darke County Jail.

Uncle John explained to Mickey that people in institutions were usually the forgotten people in society. He said they were particularly sad and lonely at Christmastime, and that is why he gave them presents. He said something that Mickey would always remember.

"Never forget the forgotten people, even if they have done something wrong. Always remember the other guy."

Mickey's most vivid memory occurred at the Darke County Jail. The prisoners' cells were in the basement, far under the old wooden courthouse steps. They led down into a dreary, musty area that contained two rows of tiny cells.

Uncle John would go down the stairs first. He somehow held his crutches in one hand, while he scooted on his behind down the stairs. Mickey would follow him trying his best to carry the gifts. He usually would make three trips from the car to the jail.

Uncle John shook hands and wished the people a Merry Christmas as he gave them their simple gifts. He would say "This is Mickey, my nephew and my helper."

The people were grateful and thankful to be remembered by someone on Christmas Eve. Mickey could see the gratitude in their eyes. He was proud of his Uncle John. He even wanted to grow up and become a man him.

This was the beginning of a Christmas tradition for Mickey. In fact, Christmas took on a new meaning for him—helping Uncle John with his rounds became the special meaning of Christmas. The experience made such a dramatic impact on Mickey that he continued it for the rest of his life.

Strong foundations are the bedrock for a lifetime of constructive values. Strong foundations move beyond being merely a strategy to becoming a way of life.

❑ STRATEGY #2:
Think Out of The Box:
Master the Art of Innovation

"More money is not what we need here because we can usually get it. What we need are more good ideas."
                                                                    –Roy Disney

Abracadabra!

A magician, clad in a black flowing cape steps onto the stage and takes a deep bow before beginning his act. He then walks over to a small table containing only a black silk hat, illuminated by a bright spotlight.

The magician looks directly at the hat and shouts, "Abracadabra! Rabbit come out of the hat." Lo and behold, the magician carefully reaches into the hat and pulls out a large, fluffy white rabbit. The applause is deafening! "How does he do that?" someone asks from the audience.

The same can be said about creating ideas. We wonder: is it really magic, or is it a specific set of techniques that creative "magicians" use to pull their unique ideas, like rabbits, out of the mind's "hat"?

The apparent slight-of-hand intrigued us so much that we wrote about the phenomenon in our book called *Think Out of the Box*. (The subject is also covered in our audio program and seminars of the same name.) We discovered in our research for the book that idea development wasn't hocus-pocus, but that it is a process filled with techniques that could become a formula for successful innovative thinking.

We use the phrase "think out of the box" to describe the process of getting out of old thought patterns into newer, more innovative thought patterns. There are certain questions that must be answered before the formula for success can be adopted. They are:

✓ 1. Do you think the same way, day after day?
2. Do people in your organization think the same way?
3. Does your organization truly produce breakthrough solutions?
4. Do you have a method to achieve continuous breakthroughs?
5. Do you have an environment that simulates innovation?
6. Do you have tools and techniques at your disposal for innovative thinking?
7. Do you have a creative thinking process?

We continue to discover unique tools and techniques that become a process and method for achieving continuous breakthrough solutions in organizations. Learning to use this process will help you to answer "yes" to the move of the seven questions above.

You undoubtedly already know that many organizations have methods, systems, and processes for controls that are often applied haphazardly, with a general lack of enthusiasm. Unfortunately, many people lack a system for innovation and the creation of ideas, preventing them from continuous improvement.

On the other hand, our research indicated that successful organizations usually follow a specific series of steps for developing unique solutions. They have a vague process that often lacks the depth required to be flexible and move fast in today's competitive rat race. Thinking out of the box is a process designed to provide increased depth by making your company agile and resilient. You'll explore major strategies for getting out of old thought patterns and into new and innovative thinking habits.

Cultures of conformity

Cultures of conformity are the biggest and most subversive enemies of out of the box thinking. They squeeze out the creative juices from everything caught in their sticky web. Just go along with the crowd, don't make waves, keep things as they are, and everything will be fine...according to them. There is no raising of the bar. There is no flexing of the Creative Muscle.

Such stifling conformity can lead to a closed mind, in a closed company, and the death of creativity.

Experimentation penetrates the shell of conformity by flexing the Creative Muscle, which we will discuss later in this strategy. If we want people to create, let them experiment. Let them try out new approaches, even if everything is going great. We have seen too many organizations that don't allow experimenting. Instead, they encourage their workers to follow the well-trodden and proven road.

We have learned to teach people how to see new and innovative solutions to a problem by exposing them to a better process. To be sure, we have some very destructive habit systems. Children succeed in school not by challenging long-held assumptions, but by going along in accepting them. Workers receive recognition at work for conforming, rather than for turning old ways of thinking on their heads.

Our children should go to school for total enrichment of their lives, not to just get by and get out! There should be innovation, creativity, and experimentation in your career, not just conformity to the party line.

Speak your mind. Present ideas. Try the new. Teachers should pass on knowledge to their students rather than being judges. Managers should improve the process rather than protect their turf.

Eliminate the boundaries

Can you imagine what Thomas Edison's era would have been like if he hadn't challenged assumptions of his day? We doubt that everyone would still be sitting around reading by candlelight because another inventor would have done it eventually if the historical contingencies were present. Can you imagine what Henry Ford's era would have been like if he hadn't learned how to challenge his people to increase their productivity—how to raise their bar? Perhaps the horse and buggy would be gone but without mass production the cost of a car would be beyond the budget of most people.

Although these inventors did not create the products they are famous for, they made these inventions better. They did not settle for the status quo. Instead, they strived to make things better by continuing to innovate and create, raising the bar, making the standards higher for people's expectations.

Innovation is the result of intelligence, sensitivity, curiosity, and experimentation, invoking growth between the head and the heart. The drive for innovation is a naturally occurring urge that can be blinded by excessive conformity. People rarely lack the spirit of innovation; what they lack are the methods, tools, and process necessary to express it, capture it, develop it, and implement it.

Do you have a process ensuring breakthrough solutions?

Many organizations have methods and procedures for accounting, manufacturing, operations, and so on. However, few systems or processes exist for continuously coming up with good ideas. This book will provide you with a process to do just that. What's more, it's easy to install!

In our book *Think Out of the Box*, we talked about our formula for out of the box thinking. The box below contains the resources, tools, methods, and techniques for thinking creatively.

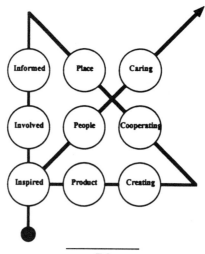

Inventors and countless others in every endeavor followed a specific process for achieving success. We've organized their principles and concepts into discrete steps you can follow. Here's a proven four-step process for success:

1. Environments and systems that involve people lead to passionate commitment because they understand what needs to be done.
2. People who are informed are the ones who are willing to cooperate because they see the vision for themselves.
3. Inspiration resulting from passion and commitment produces creativity.
4. The organization's vision and methods tend to drive these processes toward fulfillment.

This formula incorporates the same ideas:

$$\frac{I^{3+}\ P^3 = C^3}{V + M}$$

Or, in expanded form:

$$\frac{\begin{array}{l} \text{Involved + Place = Caring} \\ \text{Informed+ People = Cooperating} \\ \text{Inspired + Product = Creating} \end{array}}{\text{Vision + Method}}$$

These steps for success in innovation have grown out of the work that we've done with many companies over the years: General Electric, Johnson & Johnson, Coca-Cola, Sun Microsystems, General Motors, Motorola, WPP, and many others. These steps came from the lessons we learned in our consulting work over a period of years as we were developing projects with real people who were facing real problems at real companies. After a while, we realized that the leading entrepreneurs from the past had been using the same concepts to achieve innovation within their companies.

We've also found the need to have committed, cooperative people, who are creators. These three Cs (Caring, Cooperating, and Creating) are the foundation of the steps. As they suggest, there are three basic steps we can take to bring this about.

Step 1: Change the Workplace

Create a highly visual and engaging workplace that stimulates everyone's creativity, including customers. In this, we are concerned in the office or shop floor with the physical surroundings and design. The environment should reach out and grab people, motivate them to action, and get them excited and active by offering a work process and method that is built into the work environment. One important way to nurture creativity is this special place called a Team Center that is equipped to help people learn. Build a creativity-fostering culture, because people need a special place that has the tools required to get the job done by involving them automatically in the process. They will get involved by virtue of the nature of the environment itself. Once you've experimented with this enriched atmosphere, you'll find people becoming deeply committed to the process. We highly recommend that you try this kind of engaging workplace.

This Team Center is much like a locker room is to an athletic team. It is a resource-rich environment where people go to be informed, involved, and inspired. Then, they work to create new plans and strategies, communicate, and develop new plays before they go out and play the game. A Team Center is a creative environment that provides tools and techniques for teams to promote innovation.

A team needs a locker room—a Team Center

Athletic teams have a place to go where they can think, plan, strategize, and communicate. Without a place to gather before the game or at halftime, the team cannot do its best. Business teams need the same kind of environment.

When we are developing ways to raise the bar, we need a place where we can do the work, where we can use "out of the box" techniques to achieve breakthroughs. We need a "locker room" where members of your business team can come together is essential. We design these business-oriented "locker rooms," which we call Team Centers.

The Team Center is a place designed to create synergy and teamwork, enabling breakthrough solutions to occur. When designed into the environment properly, the Team Center can have a dramatic positive effect on productivity, communications, and overall morale. This should be a place where the team can convene to engage in innovative thinking and develop the work. Make sure your team has a plan where it can take advantage of an intellectually stimulating environment that belongs to that team *and no one else* during the time the team is working together. Avoid sending your people into a maze of adjoining cubicles for their meetings; give them a room of their own! Let this effective environment assist in making a creative climate part of your corporate culture. Call our office for more information on Team Centers.

Raise the bar when it comes to environmental design for your team. From time to time, we'll hear people say, "This is an innovation center." What they show us makes us shake our heads in embarrassment! A conference room with a few pieces of office furniture does not make for an innovation center! Boring gathering places are a little like a computer without any software, or a car without an engine.

The car without the engine

Can you imagine designing a beautiful car, all shiny and slick, with great curb appeal, but then forgetting to put in an engine? The car may look fantastic, but what good does it do if it doesn't run? However, we know people who think like this.

We often make the same errors when designing our work environments. Work environments are often shiny and pretty, but many don't have a method that makes them run. In effect, there is no engine. Instead of an improved method, we get a "brand-new same-old" thing. Nothing changes in the work environment, except the carpeting and furniture. The anticipated renewal promised by a new environment is often disappointing.

As you design a place where the desired results are creativity and innovation, you must design into the architecture a new set of tools and proven methodologies. The foundation should be prepared by teaching the tools and methods to the people who will be in the new environment. Give them the opportunity to work with the tools for awhile by applying them to a current project or problem. Let them experience the tools and methodologies working for them. Test the engine! If you like the way it runs, design the environment using it and then get in for a ride. Equip it with the products and systems that make the engine run. The Creative Thinking Association provides tools and resources to keep your creativity flowing!

Displayed Thinking

Displayed Thinking is a powerful method of visualizing and developing thoughts and ideas to come up with creative solutions. Walt Disney often said that if more people could see what they were doing, they might get better at deciding whether or not to do it! Displayed Thinking is part of the software/engine that makes your Team Center productive.

Team members need to visualize their thinking to give them a clear idea of where they are at any given moment, and how they can get to their ultimate destination. Displayed Thinking uses visuals (typically, drawings and notes mounted on boards on the wall) to tell a story that involves people instantly and build synergy naturally. People interact with visuals much more effectively than with reams of written material or endless talk.

The Displayed Thinking system is an exciting, visual work method that conveys information at the speed of light rather than the speed of sound. Sound moves at 750 miles an hour but light moves at 186,000 miles per second! Your team should take advantage of every "eyes-on" experience they possibly can. This will give them more time to listen, think and participate in lectures and other enrichment programs.

Meetings and reports are important but should not be overdone. We want to move figuratively at the speed of light rather than at a snails pace. There needs to be a pace and sense of action to get our adrenaline flowing.

We teach the Displayed Thinking system in our seminars and products to explain the key points (see an example in Strategy #7). Call us for more information on our Displayed Thinking products.

The ark of knowledge

Noah built an ark by divine direction to save human and animal life from the great deluge. It rained for forty days and forty nights before Noah sent forth a dove to see if the earth had dried up. We, too, need to build an ark and send forth doves to all parts of the earth.

We do not claim divine direction as Noah did, but we can alert you to a deluge that is occurring right now, it is the technology flood that is causing the water to rise faster and faster.

Let us build an *Ark of Knowledge* to hold what we know and will learn. Let us train doves, ready to go forth in search of land to cultivate.

One by one and two by two

Noah was given exact instructions about what to take on his ark. For us, the nature of our personalities and the nature of our businesses will determine what we take on board, but an Ark of Knowledge affords us nearly unlimited possibilities. Amazingly, the state of electronics today makes it possible to bring the entire oeuvre of humanity aboard our ark, but the extraneous fodder will test our ability to be selective.

Instructions for building an ark

Designate a space in your home or business that will serve as a physical setting to house your ark of knowledge. We call it a "Kitchen for the Mind" in the home and it can be located in an unused room or a room that serves multiple uses. We have found the living room and dining room to be excellent locations, as they are both generally used infrequently. Compare the Kitchen for the Mind with the kitchen for the stomach. We have in our homes a room called the kitchen. Technology has evolved over the years to make products that fit into this space, such as microwaves, refrigerators, ovens, blenders, crock pots, and so forth. All of these products fit neatly into this room called a kitchen, complete with recipes to make food for our stomachs.

Today, we also have magnificent technology to feed our mind: TVs, VCRs, the Internet, computers, video games, and so forth. However, we haven't created the space where they all fit neatly into the environment. Plus, we have a need for recipes (programs) to help us utilize all of these products to help us make food for our heads. In the Kitchen for the Stomach, we have breakfast, lunch, dinner, and snacks. In the Kitchen for the Mind, we have projects, programs, celebrations, and individual activities. We need to make a Kitchen for the Mind, as we have done with the Kitchen for the Stomach. We need products, programs, and celebrations to help utilize the tools in our Kitchen for the Mind. We need recipes for the mind to stimulate the mind, body, and spirit.

The Kitchen of the Mind concept is becoming more and more popular with people from all walks of life, because of changed demographics: working mothers, single parents, dual income families, and so forth. The Kitchen for the Mind is growing in popularity due to our needs to restore constructive family values and create learning environments as the population shifts to knowledge-based working. Learn more about how to put one of these exciting environments together from our "Kitchen of the Mind" audio program.

We named the Ark of Knowledge a "Team Center" in business, and it can be located in a separate space designed specifically for this use. The number of resources you need and the number of teams that may use the space determine the actual size of the room. Many Displayed Thinking walls should be placed throughout the environment to aid in everyone's development of ideas and the sharing of information. Doing so will enable others to participate more efficiently. Call us for more information about Displayed Thinking products and how to design and construct a Team Center. You'll discover how effective and exciting these facilities can be.

The purpose of the voyage

The primary purpose of our Ark of Knowledge is to develop projects, programs, and celebrations. Projects are described as those things that we are creating or working on: new products, a new marketing strategy, better manufacturing procedures, improved leadership, reduced turnover, increased bottom line, and so forth.

We can also use Team Centers for individual work, study, and creative stimulation. Your Team Center should serve as a place of renewal and refreshment.

Project example

General Electric hired us to help develop a project for improving its locomotive and for improving locomotive maintenance. The first step on this project was to set up a number of Team Centers at its factory in Erie, Pennsylvania. The master Team Center was approximately one hundred feet by sixty feet but was surrounded by several other Team Centers, including a special one in the office of the general manager, Rick Richardson. There were hundreds of Displayed Thinking boards representing the research and recommendations of the teams working on the project.

Details of the project are proprietary, however, all members of the team received extensive training on the proper use of The Displayed Thinking system through our seminars and Displayed Thinking products. They had a very dedicated leader, Rick Richardson, devoted to getting the job done and a proven method for achieving new insights in a creative environment. When difficulties were encountered, they had a strong foundation to work on solving them and were able to involve one of the group vice presidents, Carl Schlemer.

Program example

The GE management team was so proud of its people's work and its promised success, that it decided to implement a special program in order to share it with other employees in the factory and their families.

A special preview facility was set up near their Team Centers at their factory, to serve as a briefing area on the project. The preview area included the entire master plan for the project, with pictures on many Displayed Thinking boards encircling the entire room. The employees and families received invitations to an open house at the Team Center. At the open house, briefings were conducted explaining the total project and what it would mean to GE customers as well as themselves.

Celebration example

The open house further served as a celebration for those who had worked long hours on the project. The atmosphere was festive, refreshments were served, and conversation was encouraged to further build the camaraderie.

A side benefit of this celebration was the involvement of families, the community, and other workers at the GE factory. Morale and financial success were lifted to an all-time high. Rick Richardson told Mike it was one of the best-run, and most successful, projects they ever did.

Step 2: Change how you inform others

There is no strategy that is more powerful for keeping people informed and sharing information! People who are in the dark resist or distort reality. Managers who are experienced and wise encourage cooperation among key team members by sharing information with them regularly. When they are informed and in on what is happening, people will tend to be enthusiastic, flexible, and adapt to team goals—buying into the vision. Of course, some actions you may want to take are sensitive, requiring them to be kept under lock and key, so competitors don't have access to them. You may need to establish intelligent safeguards for particularly critical data. In spite of these necessary safeguards, you need to ask yourselves: Are your people convinced that your organization is trying to find a way to free up as much information as possible? Or, do they feel like outsiders in their own company? Later on, we'll discuss the "MICORBS" process, which can be utilized as a methodology to help keep people informed about important ideas and developments.

Step 3: Create something new!

Creating something new and unique is easier said than done, but it occurs every time a patent is granted. The creative challenge is where inspiration becomes a critical factor for leaders and project managers. The task is to come up with a concept or idea that no one has ever proposed before, one that will make sense and can be implemented.

To deliver those new products, services, and applications, someone has to get the inspiration! There is often confusion between the meaning of charisma and inspiration. Inspiration requires more than walking into a room and winning everyone over with your shined shoes, your gleaming smile, and your perfectly-groomed hair. If you want to create something new, you must appeal to genuine inspiration.

We know many leaders who have almost no charisma whatsoever. They are shy, introverted, and lack color. However, they too can be inspirational.

Inspiration often comes about as a result of a challenge rather than mere charisma. Charisma is nice to have at a cocktail party or social gathering, but what matters at the end of the day is the quality of performance. Delivering performance means you earn every bit of inspiration that comes your way! Inspirational leadership is earned. Inspiration cannot be bestowed; it must be earned. This kind of leadership is also an essential requirement in raising the bar.

What *is* inspiration within these parameters? The definition we like to use is simple. Inspiration is felt when someone does something so well, that his or her performance becomes a model for others. Others cannot help by be uplifted by their example.

Therefore, inspiration is linked to action, performed in a way that can cause emulation in others. This is inspiration at the deepest level.

Inspiration is also something that can happen anytime, anywhere, to anyone. We can be wearing a three-piece suit, a pair of overalls, or nothing, and be anywhere, which makes this process fun. President John F. Kennedy was the epitome of inspirational charisma, challenging America's best to plan a space mission to the moon.

Stepping out of the box

Stepping out of the box becomes part of our foundation if we want to move up to the next level of performance. The most important discoveries and solutions often come about after we have gained increased perspective by stepping back from a situation. We call this process of distancing oneself—stepping away from a system in which one is an active participant, stepping out of the box.

One constructive activity for the organizational development teams that were being developed for leadership roles at Disney World was to take each team member to visit current amusement parks that were operational. One of the famous old places they visited was the legendary Pike at Long Beach, California. This represented a typical amusement park of a far-gone era, even though it was sorely run down. Mike recalls that management and development groups had to tour the dilapidated midway, the tired carnival barkers and the seedy hangers-on.

This practice was continued after Disney World was complete so that everyone could understand what it was that Walt had been trying to improve on when creating his theme park. This was how the Disney organization reminded people of the importance of raising the bar. It reminded everyone on the team what had given rise to the theme park idea in the first place! This is one way to step out of the box you're currently in; change the physical scenery, change the assumptions, step back and find out what's out there, what is working and what isn't. The revitalization of core principles and values is established by forming a solid foundation with your people.

In order to build something that was above and beyond the traditional "amusement park," the Disney World team experienced first hand something that was less than their expectations.

Time for thinking

Do any of us have the spare time to really engage in actual thinking? When do you think? Where do you think? What do you think about? Do you think alone or do you schedule frequent participative thinking sessions? There are companies that have adopted schedules designed to allow team members to engage in regular group thinking sessions together, the same way they schedule lunchtime or break time. This is easier said than done because people who are only concerned about the bottom line will remind us of our so-called "real priorities."

It's becoming common for companies to set aside a single day out of the month (or year) and declare, "This day is our special day—today is our day to be creative." Your doctor wouldn't be particularly pleased with an exercise regimen that consisted of a jog around the block every six months or so. Thinking creatively happens spontaneously, but it also requires a regular routine, along with the tools and techniques necessary for people to harness their own creativity individually or as group members. You should have a thinking process that answers the question: "What are we trying to create or solve and how are we going to do it?" You need the regular exercise of thinking if you're going to strengthen your creativity!

Who is thinking?

Not long ago, a senior executive called our office in a state of panic. He said, "We're having problems growing our business. We need your help." Diane was curious and asked, "Who's working on solving your problems?" The answer was classic: "Nobody." Diane asked, "Why isn't anyone working on the problem?" He said, "Well, because we can't solve it."

It's sad but true. If no one is given the responsibility for solving a problem, it's going to remain an insoluble problem! This is a fact that a surprisingly high number of seasoned and sophisticated executives tend to miss. There has to be someone assigned to the task of solving a problem in order for the solution to occur! Often, it takes a team of creative, highly skilled people—people who are trained to think out of the box. We teach people how to accomplish this in our seminars, as well as in our book and tape series. As we place increasing emphasis on innovation, certain projects that need multiple fields of expertise to function require team input and team effort. No individual has the necessary resources to go it alone. To raise the bar in business, we need to learn how to function as a cohesive and unified whole.

The Creative Muscle

TM

Scientists insist on a technically strict definition of where creativity occurs—they say it is in the brain. Of course, this is physiologically true. However, we would like to embrace a broader, more figurative interpretation. We teach that creativity comes from the Creative Muscle.

Flexing the Creative Muscle can be one of the most exciting human acts if you know where the muscle is located. If you don't know, we'll tell you: It's between your ears!

In the book, we are prescribing "steroids" for the Creative Muscle. The idea is to get excited about being curious, to see an opportunity, to seize a cause, to right a wrong, and to raise the bar!

Like many other muscles in the body, people often allow their Creative Muscle to become weak and limp. Their outputs are about as exciting as last year's mission statement.

Flexing the Creative Muscle is essential for every act to raise the bar—it is indispensable when we make, produce, or design anything. Continued failure to flex the Creative Muscle leads to sterile, uninspired results that put out the flame of innovation.

The heart muscle pumps blood. Without a continuous fresh supply of blood, the heart stops its pumping and begins to die. The result is a heart attack!

The Creative Muscle gives birth to everything. Without a continuous supply of fresh challenges the Creative Muscle, much like the heart, atrophies and begins to die. The result is a boredom attack!

Thomas Jefferson, our third President, used his Creative Muscle to invent and design a variety of innovations that can be viewed at his beautiful home, Monticello, in Virginia. Jefferson had a wider interpretation of the Creative Muscle that went beyond limitations into the brain itself.

He said that personal happiness was the result of full occupation of the *mind, heart,* and *hand.* Jefferson primarily focused his creativity on the central issue of the American experiment—freedom. He viewed freedom as the absence of restraint from others, as well as government, to live your life as you choose, and from government; and especially to study and to learn whatever you choose.

Freedom, therefore, is the first requirement for being able to use our Creative Muscle. Dictatorship and authoritarian leadership restrain personal freedom, usually starting with the freedom to think your own thoughts. But, like everything else, if we don't exercise this freedom, we risk losing it. We have previously discussed experimentation—trying things out to see what can be discovered. Imagine what the world would be like if we abridged the right to create—some things would undoubtedly be worse and life would be strangled.

Experimenting with flexing the Creative Muscle begins in childhood as the baby begins to crawl. Crawling builds the inner confidence and self-esteem needed for a lifetime of exploration, making the next step of walking easier. Interrupting the crawl, forcing the child to miss toddling, leads to behavioral difficulties that often last a lifetime.

Creative thinking can and does happen anytime, anywhere, spontaneously without any preplanning or warning. Usually, an idea just pops into our head. We can be wide-awake, daydreaming, or dreaming while asleep. No one fully understands this amazing process of flexing the Creative Muscle but we learn more every day because of our insatiable curiosity. Thousands of us keep pencil and paper by our bedside tables ready to make notes in the middle of the night. Tape recorders are nearby to capture nocturnal thoughts.

Mistakes even cause us to exhibit accidental creativity. The creator, perhaps more accurately described as the discoverer, of the potato chip is a case in point. In the 1850s, a chef named George Crum from a hotel in Saratoga Springs, New York, was serving fried potatoes to a guest. The diner complained that the fried potatoes were too thick, requesting that the chef slice them thinner and thinner. Finely, fed up with the customer complaining, chef Crum made the potatoes paper-thin and salted them heavily to discourage anymore remarks.

To his surprise, the potatoes received nothing but praise from those who tasted them. People began to order and demand those delicious, thin salty slices of potatoes. The potato chip was born. Our creativity can affect us personally or it can reach world proportions as the potato chip has done. Experts estimate that over a billion pounds of potato chips are consumed every year.

The five stages of creative impact will influence how we flex our muscle in order to implement, market, or retain ideas. You need a formula. For example, Coca-Cola has a secret formula permitting it to distribute its exclusive taste on a worldwide basis. These stages are:

1. Personal.
2. Family and Friends.
3. Business and Community.
4. State and National.
5. Worldwide.

Intentional flexing of the Creative Muscle follows certain steps:

Step 1. Respond to the stimulus. The stimulus causes us to think, reflect, dream, and speculate about our response.

During the pause between stimulus and response, we conduct our research and development, form a hypothesis or tentative solutions and use brainstorming techniques to develop the concept. Dr. Jonas Salk was stimulated to work on the polio vaccine.

Step 2. Create an exciting setting. A setting or environment is selected to develop a Team Center for the purpose of exercising our creativity. Ideally, the setting should be quiet and easy to reach and dedicated solely to creative tasks and projects. If possible, it is best when it is not used for too many other activities. It should be designed to be stimulating and exciting to our senses. For example, McDonald's designed an extraordinary think tank shaped like a human brain to inspire innovation in their business.

Step 3. Think of people as the equipment that you have to work with. People are the most important pieces of equipment that we have to work with, even though we often just throw teams together with little thought. The training and development of people's creative skills and the learning of Displayed Thinking Techniques will pay big dividends to those who make the investments. We recommend training repeatedly and often, in order to master the art of creative thought.

Step 4. Establish the mood. Care and timing should be thought through from every angle to establish the mood. The mood should include selected resources, inspirational talk, and anything else that stimulates thought. We use the three M's for building mood:

1. Music (establishes mood).
2. Meditation (inspires thought).
3. Make believe (involves fantasy).

Stimulate that muscle

The only way to stimulate creativity is to seek a thrill and break out of our ruts. Humans were made to celebrate the chase, the conquest, and the excitement of creation. We are turned on by turning it on, not by retreating into a shell of conformity and complacency.

Anticipation is not a word we typically use to describe the annual strategic planning retreat for submitting, reviewing, and improving next year's budget. This is too bad, as it really should be. Read this memo from the CEO of a major U.S. company to his management staff.

MEMO

Subject: Creative Thinking Workshop
To: All Officers and Management Staff
From: Jim (CEO)

Bring your ideas, dreams, and Creative Muscle to the beautiful Pinehurst Resort for a fantastic week of pleasure, fun, and heavy lifting to raise the bar.

People believe they are empowered! We can't empower our people, but we can take it away from them. Bring your ideas to raise the bar by eliminating bureaucratic restrictions on people's power.

Technology has cut through our layers of management. Bring your ideas to raise the bar by eliminating problems through teamwork.

Manager is no longer the descriptive term that we want to use in describing leaders. Bring your ideas to "raise the bar" by eliminating obsolete language.

Let's celebrate doubling our gross next year by discovering how to be better than the best!

Flexing your Creative Muscle

Obviously, failure to consistently exercise your Creative Muscle will cause it to become weak and unprepared for use. Like any muscle, if not properly cared for and strengthened regularly, its performance diminishes. There are a number of ways to flex and strengthen your muscle. Here are a few:

Raising the stakes higher, really giving something, causes people to outperform themselves and collaterally raise the bar. For example, if we don't figure out a way to lower our costs without sacrificing quality, the cost savings will come out of your budgets. Everyone will get the message. This is called the "Big Stakes Flex," creating language that we can remember that describes what is happening.

Raising Rewards if goals are met challenges peoples Creative Muscle. You will get this big reward if you come up with a breakthrough solution. If you don't, you won't have a job! This situation causes a lot of flexing. This is called the "Reward Flex."

Facing the Consequences if goals are not met creates a considerable amount of what we call the "Stress Flex."

Unknown Opportunities or Possibilities that may lead to raising the bar give people the "Freedom Flex."

Crises cause people to deal with unusual problems that often require big flexing of many Creative Muscles. Government SWAT teams are trained to flex the Creative Muscles when called upon to act swiftly and effectively in response to a crisis. When a crisis occurs in your organization, you don't want weak muscles handling the situation. Make sure you have the right team of Creative Muscles to properly solve the problem, whatever the problems are, large or small. We facilitate many contingency projects that plan for "What if this were to happen?" What would we do? How would we solve it? These workshops help organizations flex their Creative Muscle to develop solutions followed by implementing breakthroughs that disarm and lessen the crisis. This is called the "Sweat Flex."

Constraints often push people to flex their Creative Muscle in order to achieve what is needed in spite of the limitations they have. Putting time constraints on projects or situations cause people to flex the Creative Muscle to meet the time constraints. This is called the "Box Flex."

There are times when creative people just want to flex for the heck of flexing. Go for the Flex!

Good things come from people who have strong Creative Muscles. Flex a few! Be prepared. See if your Creative Muscle is in shape.

7 ways to raise the bar through creativity

1. Ensure the freedom to experiment.
2. Be open to spontaneous creativity.
3. Capture your thoughts and ideas.
4. Avoid criticism and stay receptive to new ideas.
5. Convert mistakes to successes.
6. Plan for intentional creative thinking.
7. Have a passion for something.

We are often called upon in our work to bring in the muscle, the Creative Muscle that is, to assist organizations to Think Out of the Box. We help coach teams to Raise the Bar! We provide creative warm-ups and workouts that produce measurable results.

Principles for raising the bar: Strategy #2

✓ Make sure your mission has a method.
✓ Have a Team Center in which to think, plan, strategize, organize, and communicate.
✓ Get "software" that will make the room function.
✓ Follow a formula to thrill you.
✓ Eliminate constraints for success.
✓ Flex your Creative Muscle.

Note: *Think Out of the Box* public and customized in-house seminars and workshops are conducted by the Creative Thinking

Association of America. The popular *Think Out of the Box* book and audio series is the basis for all seminars and workshops.

Personal applications

Creating an environment for discovery

There are many personal applications of the Kitchen for the Mind. Mike's first use of the Kitchen for the Mind came to him when he was in combat in Korea. He created the concept of thinking of his army sleeping bag as a tiny room that stretched from the top of his head down to his waste line. He filled the small space with resources to improve his austere life on the front lines. He had flashlights for track lights, a pocket warmer for heat, a short wave radio, a walkie-talkie, field creations, along with books, family pictures and the ends of ammo boxes covered with paper to serve as display boards. This personal space was also referred to as a "hooch," especially in Vietnam. Later, Mike adapted this idea by converting his living room and dining room to be a Kitchen for the Mind, where his family created projects, programs, and celebrations. His audio series, *A Kitchen for the Mind*, has been sold around the world for family and individual use.

Mike's mother, Virginia Vance, died just days before he was to address several thousand people at the National HomeCare convention for our good friend Val Halamandaris, president of the association. Merritt Robinson Fink, daughter of Mike and Diane's long time friends George and Sherry Fink, was just completing a model of a Kitchen for the Mind around a dying person. It was a close replica of the Kitchen for the Mind of Mike's mother in her home in Sarasota, Florida.

Merritt's model was made of clay figures in a box about half the size of a conventional shoebox. The table revealed an elderly woman with beautiful white hair, propped upon pillows in her bed. She was surrounded by momentos from her life such as pictures of her children and grandchildren, a ceramic cat, favorite books, and so forth. There were flowers on a bedside table with bottles of her medications, and water in a glass pitcher. At the foot of her bed was a laptop computer with access to the Internet.

Standing ready beside the bed was a nurse ministering to her needs. Merritt thoughtfully placed "angel's wings" on the hospice nurse. The model was beautifully done and conveyed the dedication behind the people in the caregiving profession.

Val Halamandaris, the president of the National Association of HomeCare, proved himself a sensitive and genuine man when he introduced Mike to the convention with deep understanding about the recent loss of his mother. He thanked Mike for coming despite his bereavement.

During his talk, Mike showed Merritt's model to the audience who understood what it represented because they were the kind of "Angels of mercy" depicted in the model. He said, "We complete living wills as a standard practice of how we want our final hours of life to be. However, I believe we also need 'A living way' to accompany our living will. We should prescribe how we want to live up to the final hours. We can create a small Kitchen for the Mind around a dying person to support them through one of life's changing seasons. Their immediate surrounding, like Merritt's model, should be supportive and meaningful to the person, not just medical equipment and the apparatus of death. I would like to share with you a model of an enriched environment which my own mother experienced up until recently."

A closed circuit television camera then displayed the tiny model on a jumbo television screen high above the audience in the auditorium. It was an inspirational moment for everyone involved. One of the most important lessons learned was a personal application of the Kitchen for the Mind and the rich benefits of thinking out of the box.

❑ STRATEGY #3:
Create a Detailed Master Plan

"Most people are in the planning phase while they are executing. Many people love the results of great planning but dread the process."
-Mike Vance and Diane Deacon

A life and death lesson from dog tags

A very serious problem appeared during a fierce firefight in an infantry division during the Korean War. At first, it seemed to be minor, but as the fighting intensified the atmosphere became life threatening to the men. Anyone on the frontline was taking big risks. Casualties were extremely heavy with many solders wounded and countless KIA (killed in action). This resulted in the units being under strength or short of personnel. Vacancies were not being filled fast enough to replace the fallen men. Normally, a new replacement would come from a unit in reserve or from the replacement department, called the "repo-depos." For some unexplained reason the replacements were not coming, causing units to be undermanned, and placing them in serious jeopardy from enemy fire.

Obviously, there was either a flaw in the system someplace or someone was not following SOP (standard operating procedure). Determining the Master Plan behind this SOP was essential if the problem were to be understood and corrected. The puzzle was to locate the lag between the time a soldier was wounded or killed and the time a replacement order was received at a unit or repo-depo.

A three-man team was assigned to uncover the mystery behind the delays that were plaguing the field commanders. However, the urgency in finding the cause, coupled with tactical battlefield conditions made it almost impossible to find the original plan behind the SOP, whatever it might be. The team would have to play Sherlock Holmes by reading between the lines and then filling in the blanks from their own personal experiences.

Reconstruction of the Master Plan

The special team began their task by pinning down the purpose of their project—to find out why replacements were not being sent expeditiously to the frontline units. They reconstructed the plan using army field flip charts:

1. Replacement needed (wounded or KIA soldier).
2. Dog tags trigger requisitions:

   Each soldier wears two metal dog tags placed on a chain, one below the other, around their neck at all times. Each dog tag contained the soldier's name, rank, serial number, blood type, and religious preference.
3. One dog tag always remains on the soldier's body for positive identification. In this case, the second dog tag was a signal to start the replacement process.
4. Disposition of the triggering tag:

   First Sergeant decides where to send tag, to GRO (Graves Registration Officer), to unit personnel, to repo-depo replacement pod.
5. Requisition for replacement received.
6. Requisition filled with available soldier.
7. Orders issued assigning soldier to unit.
8. Replacement reports for duty at new unit.

The next step was to propose ideas about what was going wrong in the Master Plan. It was assumed that one of the steps was missed or that a bottleneck had occurred somewhere along the line. However, these findings couldn't rest on assumptions, but had to be verified by the organization of field studies to check each step in the chain.

This study could be conducted in two ways: Records of previous battlefield requisitions would be retrieved for analysis and review, or each case could be followed through step-by-step in the battlefield.

It was decided to speed up the research by having one team member go through the records and the other two members go right to the battlefield. They followed two soldiers who were wounded and evacuated by helicopter. Obviously, the field conditions were difficult and chaotic due to the heavy fighting.

A company's First Sergeant sent requisitions forward through channels as prescribed by the SOP. At the battalion level, the requisitions and dog tags went forward to the division level.

A master sergeant at the division headquarters was asked if he had any opinions on what might be causing the holdup in replacements. He said, "I put the requisitions and dog tags here in my bottom desk drawer until Friday. Then I forward them all together." He, like others in the system, had improvised an unfortunate new element to add to the plan.

The problem had been solved. Holding the requisitions, sometimes for as much as five or six days, was causing the bottleneck. This slowed up the replacement of new troops. A communications plan was developed and distributed throughout the division about the problem, its cause, and the solution. Here is a visual aid to show the process:

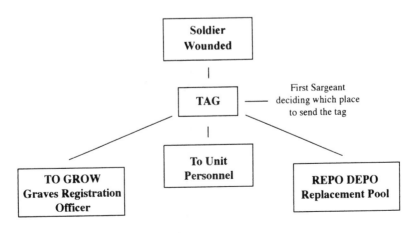

Quick thinking, excellent fieldwork, and immediate action saved lives in this combat unit. The team received the commendation ribbon for meritorious service from their commanding general.

The "dog tags" case demonstrates that when we are planning on the fly, or operating "by the seat of our pants," disaster can result. In order to raise the bar, a well thought out plan on accomplishing our mission by solving the problem should be a critical project. A strategic plan, or an overall Master Plan, for how we're going to proceed avoids the costly trap of being in the planning phase while we're executing. This can cause us to come up short or miss the target entirely.

Practical experience in creating a comprehensive, detailed plan that projects into the future is consequential. How far out into the future should we plan? We must estimate how far out into the future the plan must reach in order to have a healthy and thriving business. Envision yourself there. If you don't possess the skills to accomplish this, select someone who does have the necessary expertise and hire him or her to assist you in getting your Master Plan accomplished. A major point for raising the bar is to have an all-around Master Plan that can be authenticated by research.

Technology, needs, and trends

Innovation is driven one way or another by technology and the pressing need of a company or person. Technologies coupled with needs become the catalysts for building a new trend. Study what technologies are going to be available, understand what the emerging needs are, and you'll be capable of spotting useful trends.

One important technique in raising the bar is not always following the trends, but creating your own. Making significant strides, or causing trends to develop, enable breakthroughs that raise the bar. In other words, there must be a unique signature.

For example, Diane, Mike, and Vanessa Vance, Mike's daughter, met Marc Davis, senior Disney Animator, at the Musée d'Orsay in Paris. Davis worked on many major projects, such as *Snow White* and *Bambi*. Mike thought he recognized Marc when he saw a man looking at a painting. He was seated in a wheel-chair, which made it difficult to be certain that it was Marc, as Mike had not seen him for a quarter of a century. However, he then noticed a large blue ring on Marc's finger, a hallmark of the famous artist. Mike went up to him and said, "Marc Davis, is that you?" Marc said, "Mike, how did you recognize me after 25 years?" Mike said, "I spotted your large blue ring." "But, how did you know it was me? My looks have changed considerably in all those years," Marc said. Mike replied, "I remembered your voice. In fact," he added, "people we remember always have one or more unique features that we recognize in them."

How do we do that? How do we spot a trend, or better yet, create a trend? This question reminded us of the motion picture *Titanic.* As a matter of historical fact, there was a man who died aboard the Titanic who was an authority on the topic of trend setting. This man lived in New York City many years ago. He loaned a close friend a large sum of money to start a hat shop near Central Park in New York City. This man made it a policy to visit his friend often to see first hand how the business was progressing. Eventually, his friend fell on hard times and began to lose money, as the business was not doing well. The financier began to realize that he too was going to lose the money he'd loaned his friend. He was known for carrying around a little black book in his coat pocket. Inside this black book he placed pictures that he had taken of women who were models for the millinery shop he had invested in with his friend.

He entered into the book sketches of a variety of outfits that could be purchased at his friend's store. He then took the time to sit on a bench in Central Park and show the photos from the book to women as they passed by him. He asked these women what they thought about the various outfits. They responded with their likes and dislikes, and he wrote them down. What was he doing? Well, he was conducting one of the world's first focus interviews. This process would become standard procedure for customer satisfaction and brand building!

Eventually, he would take the comments back to his friend in the millinery shop, share them, and make suggestions to his friend about designing outfits that incorporated the elements the women interviewed wanted to wear. His friend took his advice, and the struggling shop turned around.

This man who conducted these interviews was John Jacob Astor, a man who formed one of the greatest millinery empires in the history of the United States. Astor didn't follow trends, but he created trends by seeking out the wants, needs, and desires of people. Astor's accomplishments with hat-making translate easily into a business such as entertainment.

In the motion picture business, there is a facility known as the preview house, where producers, directors, and actors can watch a film with the general public. The purpose of these sessions is to gauge the public's reaction to a motion picture—what they like and what they don't like. From this feedback, directors and producers can decide to modify a picture or even write a completely different story line. (For instance, test audiences helped producers craft an entirely new ending to the film *Fatal Attraction*.)

Or, consider the example of one prominent company. Their Team Center visualized their Master Plan by using Displayed Thinking. The plan was broken down into five-year increments for study. When they entered this room to work or to conduct a briefing, their Master Plan was in full view for anyone to see. There was immediate access to the information. It was not filed away or taken down until the next year's planning session met in Maui. Their Master Plan was arranged into three important categories. They used the acronym "TNT" to describe these categories: Emerging Technologies, Needs and Developing Trends. They evaluated each one of these categories and exhibited their effect on the overall plan. We will discuss the TNT concept in more detail later on in this strategy.

Whether you're creating a motion picture, launching a hat-making business, or rolling out any other initiative, you must first identify what people want, what they like, and what they dislike. From this information, you can create a trend by adding your own expertise.

These illustrations are not done on the fly but are accomplished by incorporating strategic thinking in the planning process. Their base line is established by the plan, which has been perfected before going to the implementation phase.

When to ride the wave

Have you ever watched surfers as they've paddled out beyond an incoming wave? What is it that determines whether they have an exciting ride or get a wave they can stay up on? The answer is clear: timing! Timing is what allows them to "take the wave." If they don't time the wave correctly, they lose it. Their Master Plan for surfing is forming as they sense the rhythm of the sea. It's the same for our personal life, but we often fail to recognize this important phenomenon.

In developing a Master Plan and strategy, one of the key challenges is understanding when to ride the wave of technology, or when to get off of a wave that's too big or not right. Most surfers, once they've mastered the small waves, go out to where they can catch bigger waves. This is an example of raising the bar that also holds true in business and in personal achievement. However, in order to take a larger wave, we have to have the timing to know when to take the smaller ones! Success is about having the patience, training, skills, and knowledge necessary to "take the right wave at the right time."

Consider the numbers of people in business you know who take waves with no training whatsoever. We know people in business who go "surfing" and haven't even taken the time to examine the shore line they'll land on after riding the wave that brings them in. This is why there is a considerable time delay between the discovery of major concepts and inventions and their final implementation—perhaps as much as 10, 15, and even 20 years!

For example, the internal combustion engine was invented 20 years before Henry Ford turned it into a huge commercial success in the automobile. After many years, the Model T still looks inviting to drive.

Electricity was discovered, but years passed before Thomas Edison developed a workable and affordable light bulb. Jim Newton, one of Edison's acquaintances, told us in conversation that Edison was often frustrated because of the slow pace of discovery. However, even with all of the frustration, Edison recounted, "The answer to solving this problem is out there—if we keep looking for it and don't give up."

The concept of the computer mouse was invented years before Steve Jobs and his Apple Computer used it on their Macintosh computer. We were working for Apple Computer at the time and Steve Jobs asked Diane to sit down at a machine while he demonstrated the mouse for her. We conjectured that the Macintosh was about to start another revolution in the way people work, and it certainly did! Roy Disney used to tell Mike and his groups at Disney, "Pick a technology wave to ride and believe in it" (see our book *Break Out of the Box*, pages 99-100, "Roy Disney's Rules for Executives").

Part of the secret for catching the wave of discovery is to study current technology and speculate and think about where is this developing. Technology stimulates further innovation! (We would like to recommend reading the book, *Innovation and The Entrepreneur*, by Peter Drucker, in which the timing technique is discussed.)

Telling the story and visualizing it

A well-executed Master Plan will tell the story about the project in a way that is easily understood. This is achieved when an effective Master Plan outlines the steps and phases along the way that benchmark progress being made in order to achieve results. If we use methods for Master Plan creation where the story is not clear, the Master Plan will be weak. Again, we don't want to be in the planning phase while executing the plan—it eats up the bottom line, cutting into the profits and the morale of the organization.

Among the ways to communicate the story of a Master Plan is to create a symbol that represents telling the Master Plan story in a visual or allegorical manner.

As you may remember, when the Walt Disney Orlando project was being built, one of Walt's strategies was to build the castle first. This approach naturally cost more money, since it meant altering the construction sequence. But to see this beautiful castle rising majestically out of the Florida swamps was awe inspiring, making it was worth every penny of additional cost. It stood erect and magnificent, alone, with nothing around it for miles.

This important strategy created motivation for everyone who was working on the Orlando project. They were simply awestruck!

Walt believed if people could envision what they were doing and the symbolism behind it, and understand the goals of what they wanted to accomplish, then the project would do well. For Walt Disney World, the castle created the dream and the vision that reflected the Master Plan.

Whenever we create our "castle" or symbol, and a dream or vision, it should reflect your Master Plan with as much clarity as possible. Additionally, you want to have a carrot that goes along with the symbol. The carrot is the reward for delivering, achieving, or reaching the goals of the Master Plan. It could come in the form of a bonus, stock certificates, or other appropriate acknowledgments for helping to accomplish the vision. Carrots and castles are the symbolic visions for any project, as well as the specific rewards for successful participation. These carrots become very significant motivators. These are practices that cause individuals to raise their personal performances to higher levels and contribute to a project. They fulfill the vision and then gain the reward.

Have a cause that drives innovation

There are often too many projects being worked on that don't raise the bar. Successful projects of any kind usually have at the heart of them a motivating cause celebre. These projects have fuel. The cause is what fires people's passion, ignites their talent and drives their motivation to implement solutions. Ken Dobler, vice president of new business development at Ehicon Endosurgery at Johnson & Johnson, exemplifies the type of leader who operates with passion. His leadership with his team begins with a major cause that drives the need to raise the bar. In developing products or techniques, they judge their work by these causes: "Will it save lives? Will it help our customers? Will it make health care affordable? Will it improve people's lives? Will it make some profit for our company?" If the project does not met the criteria of these causes, then it is not a project they would want to focus on or invest much time in.

A place to create the story

The team needs to select a place where they will develop their plans and continue to work on their project. It sounds simplistic, however, rarely is there any thought given to this needed place. If a project is complex, it may take months to develop before a plan can be implemented. It is disruptive to start creating a plan, then tearing it down, putting it up again, tearing it down again, ad infinitum. You need to designate a place where the plan can be continually worked upon and then shown to others. The Displayed Thinking system is a proven tool to develop and visualize the plan. It enables others to see where we are at any given time. This allows us to work at the speed of light. People become immersed in their work when they take advantage of a dedicated environment.

MICORBS: Building a great Master Plan

As we begin to raise the bar of performance, the strategy process we employ for creating the Master Plan is similar to that of any business plan. We also play out this process in our lives, planing household goals, trips, or parties. Today, business is embracing the boundary-free culture evolving because of newly emerging technologies. Therefore, include new functions as an addition to the traditional functions of planning, staffing, and control. We call these new functions, or formats, that have emerged MICORBS.

Most people love the results of great planning but dread the traditional processes involved. Why? Well, the process is usually very boring! However, the MICORBS process is a successful strategy for developing quick and thorough plans. We have developed the MICORBS strategy, utilizing Displayed Thinking for visualizing the details, the concepts, and the ideas. This method enables us to see where we are (or are not). It tells the Master Plan's future story. The best part is that it is fast and thorough and does not drag!

MICORBS

MICORBS is a mnemonic device for the different phases and functions of Displayed Thinking, which stands for:

Master Plan.

Idea Development.

Communications.

Organization.

Retrieval.

Briefing Boards (and Briefings).

Synapse.

M—Developing the Master Plan. This is an overview of the plan and foundation of a project. It is like an architectural blueprint for a house. You wouldn't start to build a house without a plan detailing where everything has to go. However, we often see doomed projects that start with the plumbing and usually end with frozen pipes! The "dog tags" case examined the elements in a Master Plan for requisitioning replacement personal in the military. Effective Master Plans contribute significantly to the success of any project or enterprise.

I—Engaging in Idea Development. Expand on the concepts or ideas of the Master Plan. After foundations are laid down, you need to develop and detail the parts. This is the time to figure out the parts of the plumbing. This process must be thoroughly detailed, allowing everything to flow properly. (We'll discuss this in depth in Strategy #5.)

C—Effective Communications. This entails making certain the right people are kept informed and involved. Effective communications don't just happen, they must be carefully planned by specifying who needs to know what, what do they need to know, when do they need to know it, and what media will be used to communicate it.

O—Designing an Organization Plan. This specifies determining what needs to be done, when does it need to be done, who is going to do it, and what media will be needed. This phase determines how the plan will get implemented. We often see a strong idea get generated and detailed but never come to fruition because there is no implementation and execution strategy. (The Communication and Organization plan will be discussed in depth in Strategy #6.)

R—Retrieving Ideas. This involves checking the archives for ideas and/or approaches that may have been overlooked or not yet used. Search for information and ideas from previous projects that can be tapped to see what can be learned and utilized on a current project.

B—Using a Briefing Board and Conducting Briefings. The Briefing Board System enables you and others to track where you are on the project. If there are many projects being worked on, the Briefing Boards help manage them. They help to see the status of the individual projects at a glance. Briefings also allow everyone to stay abreast of the information and give input and suggestions to the project. It keeps people informed and involved. Briefing Boards can also be used personally and at home with your family. Call us for more information on our Briefing Board products!

S—Synapse Function. Synapse is the bringing together of seemingly unrelated ideas in order to make meaningful relationships or solutions. This often means thinking through the possibilities of forced relationships or novel combinations. Joe Rolero of Ethicon Inc., a Johnson & Johnson company, often speaks of one of Samuel Morse's most daunting challenges—how to produce a telegraphic signal strong enough to send a coast-to-coast message. The problem had caused Morse many sleepless nights until, one day, he saw a team of horses being exchanged at a relay station. The solution revealed itself to the great inventor in an instant: give the traveling signal a periodic boost of power! Such breakthroughs often emerge when we try to align uncommon connections—by perceiving relationships between two separate areas of existence, or by using inversion analogies to "turn an idea upside down." (Similarly, recent advances in heart treatment appear to have benefited from the process of inversion analogy.)

Take a look at our chart on the next page to see how each of these steps works in developing your Master Plan! As you will see the MICORBS process will help move development quickly!

M — MASTER PLAN	I — IDEA DEVELOPMENT	C — COMMUNICATION	O — ORGANIZATION	R — RETRIEVAL	B — BRIEFING BOARD	S — SYNAPSE
Overview of total project needs, objectives and requirements. • Topics • Subjects • Details • Add-ons The Master Plan provides the foundation and framework for developing the project. The Project Master Plan is used to think through and list all the required subjects, details, and data that pertains to the project topic. It is the outline plan required to reach a specific, desired end result.	Idea Development is used to develop a subject or idea, usually generated off the Master Plan. It is detailed to completion. You may have many Idea Development Projects off of the Master Plan	Communications Boards answer the following questions: Who needs to know? What do they need to know? When do they need to know? Media to be used? • It is used to communicate the details of a project, event or activity.	Organizational Boards answer the following questions: What needs to be done? When does it need to be done? Who is going to do it? • All these boards may be utilized: • People Boards • Timeframe / Phases Boards • Pert Sequence Boards • It covers all the organizational details required to implement a project.	Retrieval is used to store ideas that may not be utilized at this time. • Retrieval Boards may be used to stimulate ideas. • Unused Ideas • G.P. Applications • In-house knowledge • Computer, interface with databases	A Briefing Board is a quick, effective technique used to communicate information. It is a visual "during the fact" control system. • Project Management: • Before the fact • During the fact • After the fact • Face the fact	Synapse is used to generate ideas by bringing together seemingly unrelated ideas into a meaningful purpose. It shows: Organizational Relationships • Tie-ins to other projects • Making Synaptic Connections

Use it!

As we noted earlier in the book, The National Association of HomeCare (NAHC) is led by its president, Mr. Val Halamandaris. Along with his associate, Peg Cushman, head of HomeCare University, NAHC uses Displayed Thinking in their Team Center for developing long range, strategic Master Plans that raise the bar in the health care and home care industries. Val says, "We have benefited tremendously by utilizing Displayed Thinking and using the MICORBS strategy in the development of many Master Plans."

MICORBS should guide your team assignments, too. We recommend that each function of the MICORBS process be led by a team member. Project teams that strategize the development of a Master Plan should not be too large. If the team gets too large at this phase, you often have members who don't participate and contribute. Mike suggests that the ideal number of team members is seven. His rationale is that the number seven has worked well for Steven Covey (author of the famous "Seven Habits..." books) and it worked magically for Snow White and the Seven Dwarfs. Think through each MICORBS function and assign a team member to lead each phase of the plan. Be careful who you select. Think about the Seven Dwarfs. We often see organizations put "Dopey" in charge of the Master Plan. Of course, we would recommend you pick "Doc" instead for this position.

Establish specific positions to strengthen the team

The simple act of bringing a group of people together is merely the first step in building a team. No group is able to function automatically and effectively as a team. There are prerequisites in team building which, when met, improve the chances for successful competition of the mission.

We recommend carefully selecting appropriate team members who are knowledgeable about the project. If you don't have the luxury of selecting the "A" team, then try to have *one* person on the team who knows exactly what he or she is doing! Experience indicates that effective Master Plans come from a carefully selected, knowledgeable, multidisciplined team. You don't want all vice presidents on one team. A diversified team will provide the project with a wide body of information. You may want to include an accountant on the team for two reasons: They tend to know how to fix the things that the marketing department screws up, and they give the others on the team a sense of superiority! All kidding aside, financial people tend to be creative even though they don't get credit for it. There is usually a budget or resource requirement needed for the implementation of the plan. They know where the money is stashed!

The MICORBS process serves to identify the positions for team members to play.

> ➢ Identify at least one person on that team who has the position of understanding goals the team will be trying to fulfill. If no one on the team knows anything about the project, the team will usually experience trouble. Having at least one highly qualified person on each team will insure better results.

> ➢ Identify at least one person on the team who can develop ideas and concepts into a proposal for consideration.

> ➢ Identify at least one person on the team who knows how to get the action plan implemented.

> ➢ Be sure that the team is the proper size. Just as the 1961 New York Yankees had a certain number of regular players and a certain number of supporting players, business-oriented teams must be certain that the total number of contributors is appropriate to the task at hand. It is a frequent mistake in the business world to make teams too large for the purpose of effectiveness. If half the people are folding their arms and spending every inning of all 162 games on the bench, your baseball team is too large! There is just nothing worse than people stumbling over each other.

We recommend seven specific positions for team members to play in the development of the organization's Master Plan for any creative work. For now, we want to emphasize that one of the important parts of organizational structure that makes a team a team is designating specific positions, each with clearly under-stood functions and responsibilities. Specifying positions means that everyone knows and understands the roles, limits, and expectations associated with each position on the team. Otherwise, we may find ourselves taking the field with fifteen people, each of whom becomes a self-appointed pitcher!

Team selection

Enlightened organizations select teams based on criteria that correspond to the goals of building cohesiveness and encouraging group creativity rather than as a result of power held by a favored department or internal political considerations. To raise the bar and bring your organization to the next level, be sure that your team is selected for the skills and qualifications that will help the team move toward the goal that has already been established.

For example, if your mission was to play a classic symphony, such as Beethoven's Fifth Symphony, you wouldn't pick a group consisting exclusively of oboe players simply because the owner of the concert hall used to be a professional oboe player! This would make no sense, plus it would sound horrible. Instead, you'd want to determine which instruments were required to perform the piece as written, how many people were required in each instrument category, and where you could find the most qualified players to fill the orchestra. The same basic ideas apply when you're putting together a team to solve a business problem. You must select team members thoughtfully, with your focus on the ultimate goal you've established for the team. Always keep in mind the skill levels and past experience of each team member. You must be sure that the size and composition of the team is appropriate to the task, not what might be politically correct.

Our project work has given us broad experience with teams over the years, and we've found that business situations often call for a team diverse enough to offer breadth of experience but small enough to adapt quickly to new situations. A team that is made up of seven members, as we suggested earlier in this chapter, is a worthy model. Talk to prospective team members one on one to determine if they have the interest, the time, and the desire to participate effectively as team members. In selecting a team, you need to be able to interpret both what the potential team member says openly about the prospect of joining the team *and* the subliminal signals that people send in other ways. You must be able to read and understand people effectively before putting them on the team!

As a side note, we should acknowledge super-executive Mike Jenkins's favorite formula for selecting people. He calls this process the PICI (pronounced "picky") system. He looks for people with passion for a project, integrity, commitment, and intellectual capacity. If an applicant has a four-for-four showing in this analysis, that's his kind of team member!

On a related note, our friend Val Halamandaris always makes a point of evaluating a job candidate's "CQ," or "caring quotient." He evaluates the person's "caring qualities," in addition to formal technical skills, direct job experience, or intelligence.

The art of reading people

Some time back, Mike was speaking in Wichita, Kansas, before a chamber of commerce audience that included a very bright, successful, and popular businesswoman named Jill Zell. Mike was speaking about the importance of developing a people-reading program, and he jokingly suggested that such a program was an excellent way to reach out to people you want to get to know. He walked up to Jill and said, "Excuse me, but I'm working on a people-reading program. May I read you?" People who heard the remark erupted in laughter. Without missing a beat, Jill put Mike in his place: "That's all right. I've already been read. But you can browse a little if you like!" The room exploded in laughter once again!

What is it that you really want to learn when you begin a new team relationship with a group? One suggestion for reading people is evaluating where they stand in what we call the five equities of success:

> ➤ **Physical:** What turns you on? How much do you exercise? Do you like sports?

> ➤ **Intellectual:** What do you know? What have you been reading lately?

> ➤ **Spiritual:** How do you feel about spiritual things?

> ➤ **Psychological:** Are you happy with yourself? What is your predominant mood?

> ➤ **Financial:** Are you strictly money motivated?

You can "read" someone by saying, "Listen, I'd like to read you—can you tell me how are things going? What turns you on and what bothers you?" You can ask questions about each area that you consider relevant. Too many relationships end up broken because you don't take the time to read and interact with each other on these fundamental questions.

Other equity questions include:

> ➤ For physical equity, try to find out what gets the person energized physically. Ask questions like: What kinds of hobbies excite you? What kinds of vacations do you like to take? What types of exercise do you recommend?

> ➤ For intellectual equity, try to find out what a person believes. Ask questions like: What are you thinking about or working on these days? What have you read lately?

> ➤ For spiritual equity, don't try to get a person to volunteer private information about their spiritual beliefs or practices. (That's inappropriate and sometimes illegal today, in a hiring situation.) Try to get a sense of what's important to this person. Ask: What are your guiding principles? What's most important to you? What do you think of as your purpose in life?

> ➤ For psychological equity, try to find out how the person feels about himself or herself. Ask: How do you see yourself contributing in such-and-such an area? What would you say is your biggest strength? What would you say is your biggest weakness?

➢ For financial equity, try to determine what the person's financial goals are. How important is monetary gain as a motivator to this person? Ask: Are you comfortable with what you're earning now? Are you interested in finding out ways to earn more money?

If we explore these five areas informally, we'll get a "feel" for the person that will help us determine whether they are likely to be a key contributor within the team we're considering them for. If we want greater depth, we should be willing to ask questions that illuminate the person's underlying philosophy. Ask about:

➢ **Metaphysics.** Ask "overview" questions: How do you look at the world we live in? Do you see it as essentially malevolent or essentially benevolent? Is it a combination?

➢ **Epistemology.** Ask "experience" questions: What are the most important experiences you've had in your life? (Asking this question can lead you to some really significant stories!)

➢ **Ethics.** Ask "values" questions: What are three or four ethical standards you would never break, regardless of any circumstances? (Walt Disney, for instance, was firmly committed to the ethical standard of not appropriating another person's intellectual property.)

➢ **Politics.** Ask "organizational" questions: Which do you think works best, freedom or control? (If you pair yourself with someone who's committed to control, and you're a free thinker, you will have disagreement and conflict!)

➢ **Aesthetics.** Ask "beauty" questions: What do you consider to be the most beautiful thing in life? You'll get lots of different responses. For one person, the idea of perfect beauty may be Dvorak's New World Symphony. Another's may be the face of a baby.

These are various ways to read and understand a person in some depth, approaches that will give you a clearer idea of what a person might be like to work with on a team. Of course, they're not foolproof; however, they act as a guide to help you make better choices or selections.

Check to make sure you picked the right team

Remember the powerful moment in the Broadway show *A Chorus Line* when one of the actors steps forward and asks whether or not he "is" his resume? Of course he wasn't. People are *not* their resumes. It's easy to make mistakes in assembling the team.

One way to confirm that you have, in fact, hired the right team is to conduct a powwow. A powwow is a social event at which people get to know one another and find out whether they have something to contribute to a given project. We recommend that, during the powwow, you ask the following questions. If you don't like the answers you get, select some new team members!

Powwows

Skill Inventory:
(Skills that you can bring to this project.)

Interest Inventory:
(Your general interest in this project.)

Data Dump:
(Two or three things you know that can help this project.)

Commitment:
(What is your time and interest to this project?)

Miscellaneous:
(What is the most creative thing you have done in your life so far and what was the process that led you to this solution?)

Teams and idealism

Encourage your team members to act on their idealism, not just to talk about it or pay lip service to your values.

Idealism is the pursuit of noble objectives combined with a tendency to see things as they should be. Leaving out either part of the equation is incorrect! Simply pursuing secular objectives without establishing a guiding vision for the future often leads to cynicism and stagnation. Focusing *only* on the way things should be, without any concern for the practical implications of one's ideas, can only lead to delusion and disappointment.

There is a shortage of real-world idealists as we witness in national affairs. There is a shortage of people who have the courage to maintain high hopes and the discipline to act on those hopes. Encourage the perfectionists, the visionaries, the star gazers, and the romantics on your team. Work to find a way to turn their dreams into realities that will benefit everyone.

A great Master Plan produces great results

Raising the bar in drug development

We had the opportunity to work on the development of a Master Plan for a major new pharmaceutical project. The original project manager was Tom Yonker, a friend of ours, with whom we have worked with on a number of pharmaceutical projects over the years. His company had found a protein called "Glial Cell Line-Derived Neurotrophic Factor (GDNF)." In pre-clinical studies GDNF showed promise in protecting midbrain dopaminergic neurons—the neurons whose destruction causes Parkinson's disease—from cell death. GDNF also stimulated improved function in pre-clinical models of Parkinson's disease. These were exciting findings and the company's management team decided that this was a molecule that they wanted to move into full development; they wanted to try to make it into a drug. GDNF was very unusual; it would need to be administered directly to the brain to work! The team knew right away that it would require an "out of the box" development Master Plan.

The first thing Tom had to do was assemble a diversified, knowledgeable, and committed team. He knew the team needed to include people from groups such as manufacturing, quality, and marketing, even though they wouldn't touch the molecule for years. Because of the unique challenges of chronically delivering a drug to the brain, they had to take a very long-range view of the ways in which they would manufacture the product and how many details would go into the early development requirements in the Master Plan. It was vital for them to organize the team quickly and communicate the current status of the project to them.

Tom was convinced that they needed an innovative way to get their hands quickly around the key development issues for this complicated project. The best way to do it was to hold a facilitated charrette. (A charrette is a nonstop guided workout on the development of the project; it comes from a French word loosely translated as "the bringing together of parts into one basket"). He called us to help facilitate the development of the Master Plan. We utilized the Displayed Thinking system along with the MICORBS functions as a methodology for the team to work together.

We conducted a two-day charrette, where we developed the Master Plan and started addressing and detailing many of the ideas. Afterwards, the team was debriefed on where they were at the time, listing the "to-dos" needed to get started, and the activities that needed to be completed before they met again. They put together a project time line and schedule for tasks, with due dates and each person's responsibilities for the deliverables. Several additional, facilitated planning and idea-development sessions were scheduled to assist and help speed up the work. After the team had sufficient detail to describe the development strategy to the senior management, they prepared a formal briefing on the development plan. They continued to use the Displayed Thinking system to further develop the details of the strategy and prepared detailed tasks for implementation. Everyone could *see* the plan, and the status of the project at all times. By using this visible approach, others were able to participate and provide input along with understanding of the project. People felt they had a better understanding of the project. They understood why they were doing things, had consistent rationales for making decisions, and people had an appreciation for why and how their work intersected with others. Management had a well-organized description of a Master Plan, along with an Implementation time line that people understood and were committed to. (We will discuss implementation and roll out more in Strategy #7.)

Lots of facts change in the process of drug development. Data doesn't always come out the way you hoped it would. The regulatory environment changes. Other companies' data cause you to rethink your ideas. You need to plan again, double your creative thinking efforts, and keep going! Currently, GDNF has made it into Phase Two, human clinical development. It's not a product yet, and it might never be. But two things are certainly true: It will definitely help our understanding of Parkinson's disease, and it may help uncover ways to treat this terrible disease. The GDNF project will always rank as a successful example of an effective project Master Plan. The GDNF Team definitely raised the bar for understanding how to creatively develop new drugs.

Ingredients for a Master Plan

Where do you start in building an effective Master Plan? We recommend these basic ingredients as a foundation for building a Master Plan that will lead to a successful project.

Define your purpose

Identify the motivating factors that lead to the formation of this plan. This will help underscore the reasons why you're doing what you're doing. The inability to identify your purpose may indicate that the cause isn't clear or the plan doesn't need to be created.

Establish goals and objectives

List the team's goals. Try to prioritize them and narrow them down to as few as possible. In what areas do you want to raise the bar? How high do you want to raise it? What are you trying to accomplish? You don't want to make 200 pies at once if you only need 10.

Reconfirm your core competencies

Be honest here! This will make clear what core competencies and skills you will need to accomplish the goals. Where is your baseline?

Define major issues

List roadblocks, spoilers, or show stoppers now, permitting you to go to work on them. It's better to know what they are, or what some hidden ones might be, because they could blow apart your plan.

Track down background information

What's the history? Collect as much data and information as you possibly can. Be information-rich!

Develop breakthroughs

Write down known areas that would constitute a break-through. You may have some general ideas at this point, however, we'll go to work on this in Strategy #5—Breaking Out of the Box into the Creative Zone.

Identify trends, needs, and technologies

Figure out what needs should be met. What trends are on the horizon? What new technologies will affect you? What existing technologies can you transfer to your business?

Create unique factors

Develop differentiators that help you to raise the bar and separate you from the competition. How do you know when you have a unique factor? Well, you've got a unique factor when people have to go to you to get something and you're the only one who has it.

Resources required

You might not know all the resources that are required at this time, but don't forget this category in the plan. It's important to know *up front* that you have limited resources (people, technology, or funds) to work with on the project.

Design a timeline

When will you want to start rolling this plan out and what are your target dates? Some people put together magnificent plans but have no plan to do anything with them! Once you have a timeline, try to figure out how you can expedite the project.

Determine your measurements

Figure out how you will determine whether you've reached your goals. What mechanism will you use to assess your progress toward and achievement of the goal?

Miscellaneous

Always have a miscellaneous category to put up ideas and concerns that may not have or need a specific category, but should not be lost.

These are just a few standard subject categories for your Master Plan to include for raising the bar. In Strategy Number Five, we'll discuss how to develop and detail the ideas off this Master Plan. Then, in Strategy Number Seven, we'll show how to implement and roll out your plan.

Fear of the dark

Overcoming the fear of the dark, or the unknown, will help us to get out of the box and to raise the bar. You need to overcome the feeling that you're alone with no support. You need to overcome the fear of the unknown and of going beyond. For almost everyone, from the youngest child to the oldest adult, it is the fear of "the dark" that will keep progress from happening. It is what prohibits you from raising the bar.

Fear of the dark, of unknown places where light hasn't penetrated, stops people from creating. This fear stops people from doing the quality of work they're capable of doing. It stops them from doing what will help them develop the techniques that will lead to success.

A classic story about the dark comes from the ancient Greeks. We'd like to recommend that you read Plato's *Republic*, Book Seven, which contains the "Allegory of the Cave." If there ever was a story illustrating the terrors of the dark, and how to find a way out, it is this famous passage from Plato's philosophical masterpiece.

Here's a synopsis and one interpretation of the plot. Humanity has been put into a giant cave and chained down to the floor of it making movement impossible. People are in bondage. It's dark in the cave, except for the lights coming in over the shoulders of what is meant to be humanity. The lights are shining on the walls of the cave and people can see shadows on the walls. They wonder about the light shining on the cave walls, even though they cannot actually see the lights that are casting the long shadows.

When people are in the dark and someone shows them the light, it naturally arouses their curiosity. It stirs their motivation. Therefore, to get out of the dark, one of the first things we have to see is a glimmer of light. We have to see a glimmer that entrances us, that stimulates us, that gets us on what we call the "streetcar named desire."

In the "Allegory of the Cave," humanity picks one person from the group, someone who is a competent reporter, to go out and investigate what's causing the light. This was Plato's equivalent to what we would call "research and development" (R&D) in modern corporate terminology.

In R&D, we pick a team of people to go out and explore what is (or is not) causing a certain phenomenon, return with the information we've collected and the resources we've developed, then tell the rest of the company what is out there.

In the story, a person ventures out and makes a startling discovery—that the shadows on the cave walls are the effect coming from the sunlight. Try to imagine what happens when this person goes back and tells people about the giant ball of fire hanging in the sky! Of course, they don't believe him at first. At first they think the R&D person, the reporter, is absolutely out of his mind! They figure they sent out the wrong person to report the findings. They then send another person out to confirm what's really out there. And lo and behold, the second person confirms that the first person really did see a huge ball of fire hanging in the sky.

Master Planning, as a process, brings each of us into the light, or into enlightenment. Enlightenment is when we have enough knowledge, and enough resources, to develop a plan that tells a story and will keep us out of the dark. Although this is only one interpretation of this classic, it can help you raise the bar—by moving into the light!

The gap

We have referred to the Techno-Psycho Gap cutting its way through our culture. It is more threatening than the San Andreas Fault and potentially bigger than the Grand Canyon.

We are living in an era of technological abundance and psychological poverty. Individuals have the power of super computers available to them, but they feel strangely impotent and ineffective, despite the obvious technological advantages at their disposal. To quote Charles Dickens, "It is the best of times, it is the worst of times."

"Cultural lag" has been the nemesis of the late 20th century. The Techno-Psycho Gap could be the nemesis of the early 21st century. The "culture lag," in sociology, is the failure of one part of a cultural entity, such as major social institutions, to keep pace with the changes in other areas, such as scientific advances.

The Techno-Psycho Gap is caused by a widening disparity between people who understand and use technology and those who remain ignorant of it, as we discussed in the introduction by comparing electronic literacy with literacy.

Our response to the Techno-Psycho Gap will determine the quality of life for us and for generations to come because it accentuates elitism. Therefore, it's important to understand the social conditions the gap has created and its continuing impact on world culture. Broadly speaking, too many decision-makers are stuck with one foot in the past, while moving into the future with their eyes on the rearview mirror. This practice prevents people from making breakthroughs and finding solutions to problems; they "play it safe."

It's frustrating to observe people attempting to solve problems by applying the same old tired solutions, when innovation, originality, and raising the bar are desperately needed. But there's a paradox. Here we are in an era where sand, glass, and air as fiber optics, silicon chips, and radio technology can usher in an economy of abundance for the world. All too often we're still talking about things like scarcity, horsepower, and whether or not we should start a quality program in our business. We're not using all the tools at our disposal—we're widening the gap!

For example, thousands of moderately skilled and unskilled workers are being replaced by technology-oriented workers who require more training, education, and experience than they have. Adding insult to injury, we're importing workers from other countries, rather than training and developing our own people. We need a Master Plan to change this and raise the bar.

How we do this should be top priority, because if we don't solve this problem, the good old United States of America will be up the proverbial creek without a paddle. There are four central issues surrounding the Techno-Psycho Gap that we can do something about, four areas that should be considered carefully in Master Planning for the future. They are:

1. Career and job opportunities.
2. Education and knowledge.
3. Happiness and fulfillment.
4. Social issues and problems.

1. Career and job opportunities

Technology has created thousands of new jobs, but thousands have also been eliminated. Downsizing and outsourcing have wreaked havoc in the workplace. Tragically, we've not planned effectively for handling this massive displacement. This is the result of not having an effective Master Plan...or any other plan, for that matter.

Careers and job opportunities are not only essential for people's livelihood and security, but also for providing them with a sense of pride, a sense of belonging, and a sense of achievement. Instability causes psychological problems and a sense of failure that which in turn leads to a life crisis, and if deep and broad enough, a national crisis.

Recommendations

Prepare yourself and those you influence for careers that still exist. Many colleges are still training people for careers that don't exist. People are still enrolling in hundreds of career training courses at hefty fees for jobs that have already disappeared or are disappearing fast. Prepare by developing skills in pace with developing technologies. Avoid training for jobs where there is little hope or diminishing opportunity.

Raise the bar! Prepare yourself and those you influence to develop the entrepreneurial spirit and build new opportunities. Today, successful people act independently and tend to be self-motivated. Create career opportunities for others by responding to needs and unsolved problems. The career and job opportunity issue is so large that it will require the efforts of many people and many creative entrepreneurs will need to be among them. However, the door of opportunity is wide open because nearly everything either needs fixing or can use some improvements.

2. Education and knowledge

A good education, usable knowledge, and the dedication to a life of continuous learning are essential for success and survival. The need for continuous learning is a critical issue that requires a complete reevaluation of how most of us use our free time.

In a sense, we can never really "graduate" from anything. Our system of rewarding degrees and diplomas may well be sending the wrong messages to the young. Perhaps we should each be born with three doctorates, four master's degrees, and two bachelor's degrees attached to our birth certificate. The more we know and learn, the more degrees are removed from our names, so that the best educated have the fewest degrees! Current technology has introduced an entire new set of skills required to get along. Those who have not kept up with the advances feel out of touch, disconnected, obsolete. We deride these persons by saying, "He's out to lunch."

Recommendation

Shift your emphasis to an intellectual life of growth and continuous exploration of new knowledge (if you haven't done so already). Ask yourself: What are you focusing on? It's easy to get our priorities messed up in this society. We rarely see people lined up in the morning for tickets to a lecture or a seminar, but we see them lined up for rock concerts and sports events. We must not forget to stimulate our brains!

Embrace the lifestyle of the self-taught person, the autodidactic. Design a Master Plan for your life that includes the five equities that we talked about earlier: physical equity, intellectual equity, spiritual equity, psychological equity, and financial equity.

3. Happiness and fulfillment

The Constitution gives us the right to pursue happiness, which some leaders really take to heart. Technology has given us the tools to enjoy life on an unprecedented scale. However, those who have not kept abreast have been caught in the Techno-Psycho Gap and feel diminished. Fulfillment is when our dreams, goals, and objectives are met with success. The unfulfilled person is nearly always the unhappy person. Happiness usually is a by-product of fulfillment.

Recommendation

Simplify your life, but don't get complacent about the important issues. Remember, simplicity and striving for excellence are the essential concepts that must also be applied to what will make us happy. There is considerable fulfillment when we see ourselves growing and developing into what we want to be—the development of our potential. The new drug on the market, Viagra, is making many people happy for this exact reason—it develops potential!

4. Social issues and problems

Technology is a double-edged sword pertaining to major social issues. The quality of life has been vastly improved on the one hand, but it also has been diluted. Medical advances, complex diagnostic equipment, and powerful healing drugs have helped us control pain and suffering and improve people's lifestyles. Life spans have been extended, but so have crowds, pollution, noise, and many other challenges to the quality of life.

No one can measure the cost of stress placed on the individual because of the rapid pace of change in our culture. But the impact of mass media resulting from the technological wonders of television, the Internet, and other media is truly staggering. The digital revolution will continue to bring about even more social change.

Recommendation

Take on a cause and work for it with passion. Take on a problem and devote yourself to finding a solution. You will feel more fulfilled—and you'll help turn the world into a better place.

For example, we got involved with Avon Products Chairman, Jim Preston, and Former Group Vice President Phyllis Davis, in a wonderful cause to participate in the restoration of the Statue of Liberty during Avon's 100th Anniversary. This cause generated a great deal of passion from Avon employees and customers.

We got involved, pushing our passions for the betterment of others. Mike helped start orphanages for displaced children in Korea, which got others to do the same. Diane has been on the board of the Caring Institute, which helps her fulfill her needs to help others.

Social responsibility and challenge

The social responsibility for these four major issues in the Techno-Psycho Gap belongs to all of us. The challenge is to close the gap by raising the bar and correcting the problems.

Walt Disney used to say, "Each person's story is potentially a bestseller if we exercise whatever given talent we do have." Some people are blessed with more talent than they could ever use. But every person has something he or she can do to make a contribution. The time has come for us to get on with it. The time has come to stop complaining and start creating. The time has come to start contributing our time, our talent, and our creativity to close the gap and raise the bar.

A clear and simple Master Plan

As you start to develop your plan, you'll want to stimulate as many ideas as possible. As you continue to develop the details of your plan, you'll have breakthroughs that will suggest revision to the plan. After you have developed the details of the plan, go back and fine-tune what you've come up with. Simplify it. Remember, a well thought out plan should tell a clear story. Allen Weiss, Ph.D., speaker, consultant, and author of many great books, such as *Best Laid Plans—Turning Strategy Into Action Throughout Your Organization*, reinforces the fact that you need to have a well-thought-out plan in order to expedite it and get it successfully implemented.

How to expedite the plan and a project

Certain projects require quick solutions, especially when time is a critical issue. Getting new products and services to the marketplace is essential for the success of many organizations. In these situations, you need to develop a plan *fast*. To develop a detailed, thorough Master Plan fast, we recommend the team conduct a charrette. This is the process of gathering facts, background information, creative concepts, innovative approaches, and so forth, that can eventually produce a workable solution. These creative sessions should be facilitated to conclude with a preliminary Master Plan.

Gather the many pieces of the puzzle and go to work on piecing them together. Charrettes keep us focused, give us a workout, and keep the process going until we achieve breakthroughs. Many companies avoid devoting six to eight months on developing a Master Plan because of costs and scheduling. What is popular now are off-site charrettes where groups will work non-stop for two to three days, (sometimes a week) until the Master Plan is complete. One deliverable of a charrette is to end with a Master Plan story.

We facilitate many charrettes for the development of Master Plans, particularly for overseas projects. This approach is well-suited for two reasons. First, the approach is quick and enables people to move almost immediately to implementation. Second, everyone is usually from different countries, which prevents them from traveling back and forth each month. Resuming where you left off last will cause long delays. Logistics make it necessary to get the plan done in a short, concentrated period of time. Stop fooling around: conduct a charrette and get the plan done! We will discuss how to get the plans implemented in Strategies #6 and 7.

Principles for raising the bar: Strategy #3

✓ Develop a detailed, thorough, and inspiring Master Plan that tells a clear story.

✓ Get the Master Plan done so you can move it into action; don't belabor the process.

✓ Don't execute while you're still planning.

✓ Think through all the short-term and long-term aspects of your plan.

✓ Pick the right team members.

✓ Give team members specific positions to play.

Personal applications

A plan to remember

The Brain Exchange is a monthly audio magazine that we have produced for many years. Each month, subscribers receive a program, that features discussions by Mike and Diane on creativity, leadership, values-based management theory, and breakthrough solutions—as well as questions sent in from subscribers. We suggest resources for the purpose of enriching life during each session. These include books, important articles, reviews, electronic innovations, and other activities.

One such activity was aimed at parents by recommending what they might do to celebrate a child's 21st birthday. It was an example of a Master Plan for a special celebration honoring someone in your life that you love.

The following is the plan we proposed for this special occasion:

Itinerary for Child's 21st Birthday Celebration

First Day:

- Fly with your child to New York City. Arrive around noon. Have a limo pick you up.
- Go to your suite in a luxury hotel, which you have reserved for three nights.
- 4 p.m. Have snacks and drinks at the hotel's restaurant, just off the main lobby. A live string orchestra entertains the guests. You may even run into a few celebrities!
- 6 p.m. Return to your suite for the purpose of grooming for the theater.
- 7:15 p.m. Hire a limo to take you to the theater and wait to pick you up after the performance.
- 8 p.m. Arrive just before curtain time at a theater for a hit musical production. Get the best possible seats from a ticket broker.
- 10:30 p.m. After the show, your limo driver will be waiting in front of the theater.
- 10:45 p.m. Supper at a famous restaurant. Tip the maitre d' generously when entering and your service will be perfect in every detail.
- 1 a.m. Limo returns you to entrance of your hotel.
- 1:15 a.m. Ask the doorman to hail you a horse-drawn carriage for a short ride in front of Central Park.

Second Day:

- 12 p.m. Sleep until noon. Have room service deliver fruits, coffee, and champagne. Look out the window, read the headlines, and talk with your child.
- 2 p.m. Limo picks you up for a quick tour of the Guggenheim Museum, followed with a drive-by of the UN and a ferry ride to the Statue of Liberty.
- 4 p.m. Go to a touristy restaurant (such as Tavern On The Green) for an early dinner.

> ➤ 6 p.m. Walk down Fifth Avenue and buy your child a special and memorable gift.
> ➤ 8 p.m. The rest of the time is your own. We think you have the idea of our Master Plan. Have fun!

We were having a late lunch in the Palm Court at the Plaza Hotel in New York City with a client and a man yelled across the room "Mike Vance, is that you?" The restaurant was crowed with people who gazed at the exuberant man. Mike was a little taken back as the man rushed toward him. Diane was wondering what had Mike done now!

The man said, "Mike, I'm a subscriber to your *Brain Exchange* magazine. This is my daughter, Mary. It is her 21st birthday and we're doing exactly what you said to do on that *Brain Exchange* tape. We're going to see the Broadway show *Barnum* tonight."

We were flabbergasted, to say the least, but we were pleasantly surprised that someone actually did what we suggested on the *Brain Exchange* program. We wished his daughter a happy birthday and reaffirmed how wonderful the *Barnum* musical was. We suggested that perhaps we would all see each other at the St. James Theater.

The evening's performance of *Barnum* was highlighted by an extraordinary encounter with the man's daughter during the intermission. She walked over to Mike with a big smile on her face, hugged him, and said, "Mike Vance, I don't have the slightest idea who you are. I don't know what you do. I never heard your name until this afternoon at the Plaza Hotel with my dad. He and I have never been really close until this trip, which he gave me for my 21st birthday. In fact, I've never done many things with him at all until this beautiful trip. We went camping as a family several times but he was always fishing or playing cards. Whoever you are, I want to thank you, because my dad said that you suggested that he do this with me. This is a special time with my father that I will never forget. Whatever it is that you do, don't ever stop doing it."

We have never stopped doing these things or making these suggestions. *The Brain Exchange* magazine provides resources, recommendations, and insights for creative thinking and living and we hope it contributes to people's lives just as it did for Mary.

❏STRATEGY #4: Develop People to Become Pathfinders

"You can't grow beyond your good people."
–Andrew Carnegie

Training someone to do something new

Some trainers use a "macho mentality" that reflects a "sink or swim" attitude. Trainees are put immediately into a test situation to see if they can survive the challenges they face. Another approach is the experimental approach: trial and error. Trainees experiment with a task (trial), study their mistakes (errors), and try again.

Now, if we're learning to, say, fly an airplane, there are minimum standards to follow, such as requiring an instructor to be present in the plane at all times before you can solo. We can't employ the sink or swim method, but we can use trial and error in the presence of a flight instructor.

Mike will never forget his first flying lesson at age 16 at the Fort Hamilton, Ohio, airport. Mike and his instructor, Joe Hogan, took off in a Cessna 120 and climbed to 10 thousand feet for level flight. Joe took his feet off the rudder pedals, took his hands off the stick, and said to Mike, "Fly the airplane."

Mike tensed up. Joe grabbed the stick and pulled it suddenly all the way back against his chest with considerable force. The nose of the little plane began to pull up, steeper and steeper, until a loud horn sounded in the cockpit—the stall horn. The nose was up, the tail was down, and Joe violently kicked the left rudder pedal, causing the plane to roll over and start falling straight down in what's called a spin. The ground rushed toward them at ever increasing speed.

At that moment, Mike decided to give up the idea of flying lessons. Joe shouted, "Mike, take the controls. Fly the plane out of the spin. Don't over control. The plane will almost fly itself out with just a little help on the stick."

Mike repeated these lessons with Joe Hogan for ten hours during the next four days, practicing takeoffs and landings, planning for other emergencies, and so forth. Then, early one morning, they took off to fly the pattern around the small airport: downwind, base leg, and final approach. Upon landing, Joe told Mike to pull over to the side of the hanger. He jumped out, yelled, "Take off solo!" and slammed the door behind him.

If you ever learn to fly, pilots will tell you that the most thrilling experience of your life will be the solo flight, because from this point on it is sink or swim, you're in charge. You're on your own.

We wish that every person who is responsible for training anyone to do anything could take flying lessons, because the protocols for training are superior. The discipline, techniques, and procedures learned in flight training transfer to many other tasks.

Good judgment becomes a major requirement for parents, teachers, and leaders in deciding on the actual methods to be used in training and developing people.

It would be a disservice to you to oversimplify this monumental responsibility by offering pat answers or suggesting that you try to follow "magic formulas." Therefore, we offer these ideas on how to train as suggestions for you to consider incorporating into your arsenal of tools for helping people to grow and fulfill their potential. This is an important task. We don't want our students to crash and burn; we want them to soar to new heights.

The test is to prevent trainers from wasting time and resources on a person who is not trainable in a given area. People often spend too much money and time on people who, for one reason or another, simply aren't going to make it. You must develop a test or criteria to determine when you stop the process of training because it is hopeless. This then enables the person to begin training in a field where they can be successful.

Joe Hogan, the flight instructor, later told Mike that the critical judgment that needed to be employed occurred when they went into the spin. He said that a trainer has to use such situations to determine whether a prospective student has what it takes to become a pilot. There must be a test! "You had to assume the controls, even if you were reluctant," Joe said. Fortunately, Mike had "the right stuff." He passed that test.

Revival of the fittest

Buckminister Fuller, the ingenious inventor of the geodesic dome, had the amazing ability to capture very complex ideas by compressing their parts into a statement that you cannot easily forget.

Fuller demonstrated this faculty one evening when we were having dinner with him by making an observation about the abilities of we mortals that stimulated our imaginations.

He said, "We humans in the universe are designed for complete success. All we need is a revival." He used revival to mean rebirth and resurgence of our best values, our talents, and our highest motives—a renaissance of the spirit.

Fuller believed, along with many other learned persons and scholars of anthropology, that we were designed to survive life's demanding vicissitudes as among the very fittest of all species. He observed at dinner, "If we study the body and brain from the point of view called total comprehensive design science, we're made for complete success."

Buckminster Fuller loved and celebrated human potential, its promise, and its creative power, which you could feel by being close to him. He often commented that he had lived his entire life as an experiment to discern just what one person could do with his life. He insisted that today we need a revival in our belief of what one single individual could accomplish. We often uphold the value of animals and rocks more than we uphold the value of persons.

Consider the awesome power of a single person by recalling the activities of these contrasting pairs:

> ➢ Da Vinci and Napoleon.
> ➢ Gandhi and Hitler.
> ➢ Lincoln and Stalin.
> ➢ Dr. Salk and Dr. Jekyll.
> ➢ Disney and Dahmer.

The herculean power of just one person is mind-boggling. The scope of personal empowerment is seemingly unlimited. However, Fuller was not a Pollyanna observer or a cockeyed optimist about the escalating problems society faces at every turn in the road. He was firmly reality-based. He believed that people could achieve most anything, if their goals were within the realm of truth. The price to achieve unbelievable dreams is the revival of realistic thinking to replace wishful thinking.

Realistic thinking is what uncovers operating general princi-ples in the universe that are applicable to our problem. Realistic thinking reveals the truth; therefore, realistic thinking creates the conditions for honesty and understanding of the true facts. Real-istic thinking provides us with a revival credo.

Revival occurs when we respond honestly to needs. Honesty is adherence to the truth, truth is the discovery of reality, reality is the discovery of the operating general principles of the universe.

This fact is why Thomas Edison once said, "I've never invented anything, really. I discovered it out there. The answer is out there if you keep looking for it..."

It's time for the revival of long-range thinkers instead of short-range opportunists. The world needs a big vision, a big dream, and a big challenge to replace the obsessive preoccupation with the immediate bottom line and short-term exploitation.

We think Walt Disney summed it up best when he said, "Think beyond your lifetime if you want to do something truly great. Make a fifty-year master plan. A fifty-year master plan will change how you look at the opportunities in the present."

Revival of ethical creativity and originality

The most fundamental challenge is not merely the revival of creativity, but the revival of ethical creativity and originality. As we noted in listing contrasting pairs like Gandhi and Hitler, both exercised creativity, but one was based on ethical values and one was based on immoral values.

Now is the time to revive ethical values, which are constructive, to drive our creativity. In fact, more originality becomes possible when we abandon unethical practices because originality comes from the discovery and uncovering of truth.

There is often too much sameness, too many cookie cutter operations that employ knee-jerk, predictable solutions to problems. The solution to every business problem should not be the elimination of people, but rather a creative redeployment of human resources. We need to revive the concept of loyalty to the company and loving the place we work. Every executive laments the loss of loyal employees. However, it's a two-way street. The executive builds loyalty to a company when the company is loyal to the employee.

Truly innovative product discoveries are a result of the company's performing at its optimal creative level where the organization and the employees work in harmony with each other. We need those kind of innovative products that cause us to drool for them, products that we salivate over, because we've got to have them *now*.

Remember the first little Ford Mustang that multiplied faster than rabbits? Remember the original Lincoln Continental with the spare tire molded into the trunk, which causing people to stop and stare?

Do you remember the days when it was actually a goal to be among the first persons to have a certain new product? For example, a color television set, a videotape recorder, a microwave, a cellular telephone, a multimedia-capable computer with DVD, and once, even an automatic garage door opener.

So the fundamental question is the revival of "what" and "for what"? Revival of the fittest is about the revival of leadership qualities that promulgate ethical creativity and originality. It's about leadership qualities that get both immediate and long-term results. It's about coming through with flying colors. It's about raising the bar and developing people.

A pathfinder

A pathfinder is a person with a vision who will get you where you want to go. Pathfinders often have some of the same attributes as visionaries—they have passionate feelings and total commitment to their cause. However, the visionary may not bring the plan to closure. A pathfinder does! Pathfinders lead the way to raising the bar.

Pathfinder characteristics

Some people are pathfinders. Many have the ability to be pathfinders, but don't know it.

Frank J. Ponzio, Jr., CEO of an information technology service company, has been a leading pathfinder in his field for years. He has had the opportunity to meet and work with many businesses' senior managers whose organizations are leaders in their fields. In talking to Frank about his experience in working with pathfinders who have raised the bar in their organizations, he is in agreement with many of our Creative Thinking Association members.

Check the characteristics and attributes of pathfinders (listed below) and discover if you are one.

➢ Pathfinders know how to develop a detailed plan of action. They create a realistic dream and vision.

➢ A pathfinder also knows how to sell a vision. They know how to get "buy in" and acceptance from others.

➢ A pathfinder has the courage to break away from popular thinking, to set a different course, and to take risks.

➢ Pathfinders break out of the crowd. They are often iconoclasts. They usually take the first step.

➢ Pathfinders test the limits. They break new records.

➢ A Pathfinder is decisive. Pathfinders are willing to modify decisions when required. Pathfinders often conclude that they need to change in order to reach the goal. This doesn't mean failure, but an ability to adapt to change.

> ➤ Pathfinders have perseverance to overcome obstacles that occur, the distractions that arise, and the determination to finish what is started.

> ➤ Pathfinders seek out and get to know the facts of what is and is not happening, assess the impact on the business, and support decision making for risk management. They are rich in the information category.

> ➤ Pathfinders have the freedom to explore and experiment.

> ➤ Pathfinders show others the way. They mark the trail.

> ➤ Pathfinders create the model by marking the trail and showing others the way by creating new traditions.

Steve Steffke, a friend and associate, has been a leading pathfinder in the transportation industry, among many others, throughout the years. He shared his knowledge about what has led to many successful projects using these tools and techniques. Steve has demonstrated that pathfinders keep the creative spirit alive and growing by creating a collaborative, visual work environment where people are able to grow, develop and contribute. Pathfinders involve and inspire people, raising the bar of their capabilities and training them to the next level.

How do you find people with potential?

Often, Walt Disney would drop in on a team that was working on a project and spot someone that he sensed had high potential. Walt would say, "Take him out of here and put him over there, so we can develop him further."

An example of spotting potential in people comes from a major motion picture studio, and it's not meant to be sexist. The studio wanted to identify a cadre of future leaders in the film industry for the purpose of recruiting and management development. The normal procedure would be to go to the school and ask the dean for recommendations of outstanding students. The dean would always tend to choose those who knew how to play the game of politics. Consequently, the profiles were always the same, and the dean usually missed the dynamic student who had true potential.

Therefore, the studio developed another approach for finding candidates for their program. They selected the four leading sorority houses on the campuses of universities with film schools. They then sent an after dinner speaker from their studio to the sorority who would win their confidence. The speaker then invited the women to identify five or six men on the campus that they believed had the potential that the studio was looking for. And, of course, the joke was these women knew who these men were because they were after them. Their judgment was based on something deeper than making good grades! It was noted during the duration of this creative recruiting program that the profiles of the men selected by these women were outstanding in every way.

A group of over 100 candidates were recruited and entered the program. A dozen men, a very high number, became leaders within the film industry. This was an example of raising the bar and getting out of the box in order to recruit an individual of high potential.

You can also spot a person with high potential where Displayed Thinking and briefings are being utilized because you can *see* the skills of people as they work visually. These are powerful tools for picking winners.

When looking for these pathfinders, it's best to keep a detailed definition of what a pathfinder is and what he or she can do for you. Here is a simple reference to finding someone that is better than the best.

What is a Pathfinder?

1. Pathfinders see the vision—they dream/reach out/ break out of the crowd/are iconoclastic.
2. Pathfinders create the plan—develop the master plan/must have the freedom to explore/experiment/tick people off.
3. Pathfinders take the first step—they test ideas and limits/ break new records.
4. Pathfinders show others the way—they mark the trail.
5. Pathfinders create the model—they keep raising the bar.

Train for all "As"

As a former dean of Disney University concerned with training and people development, Mike learned that to raise the bar of performance you have to have willing people and you have to invest in the best training program possible. The task was to train thousands of hourly workers and hundreds of people for management and leadership roles, in order to grow the Disney organization to support the Orlando project in Florida.

Walt Disney believed that good training produced even better results with people. His standards precluded having "B" and "C" students operating Space Mountain with thousands of people going upside down in the dark. Our challenge was to have "A" students running the operation. This was a pedagogical challenge. How do you have all "A" students?

Integrated didactics

"Integrated didactics" is a new concept that brings together resources that are meant to teach and instruct others. This discipline was inspired by the work of Dr. Maria Montessori. This innovative teacher invented didactic teaching materials for the classroom and broadened the meaning of "didactic" to cover anything that is "meant to teach."

Integrated didactics promote synergy between the resources and the participants in a project, allowing all components to work together to achieve a common goal. For example, creative environments such as the Team Center bring together all the resources, materials and tools necessary to develop specific projects in a designated location, whether it is a boardroom, a locker room, or a kitchen. The components of integrated didactics should include the Displayed Thinking system, reference materials, model building supplies, computer resources, communication links, and so forth.

Frank Lloyd Wright enriched the physical environment

We have learned these lessons through exposure to the ideas of Frank Lloyd Wright, Walt Disney, and Buckminster Fuller. In many of our seminars, we discuss Frank Lloyd Wright's philosophy about design. Mr. Wright believed that many of us live and work in sanitary slums, that our environments are sterile and need to be enriched.

Walt Disney helped people to gain skills

Walt Disney believed that people would act and perform according to the environment in which they have been placed. People often fail because they lack the skills to succeed in their environment. People will stay in environments where they are learning and leave environments where they are not learning.

Buckminster Fuller introduced superior methods

"You don't change the old by resisting it, or fighting it, you change it by making it obsolete through superior methodology." Fuller pointed out that people often resist and fight change because what it promised was not made good on. This always leads to disappointment.

Places, people, and products

At the Creative Thinking Association of America, we use integrated didactics to work with many companies on a wide variety of projects. Those who have worked with us have experienced this holistic approach to a project. When working with a company, we begin by setting up a temporary environment for a Team Center to help organize the components and resources. We place special emphasis on these three basic areas: the place, the people, and the product. Let's review each one again:

The Place: A physical environment in which people (employees or customers) are immersed called the Team Center. The design and creation of this space is the outgrowth of asking questions such as: What do we want to have happen in the Team Center? What do we want the space to achieve? What do we want the space to do for the people?

The People: What do the people want and need in relationship to their assignments (thinking about both current and future needs)? How can we design the environment to improve performance? What would enhance what is done in the environment? What will be the working methods and the ongoing training systems operative with the space, now and in the future? How will people communicate in the space? Is it effective or can we improve upon its design?

The Product: What is the product or service that is, or will be, produced in the environment? What is needed to achieve the highest quality product or service? What will be our creative thinking process?

Often, when we move to a new office, home, or corporate facility, we experience an example of what can happen if integrated didactics are not applied to the move. We constantly hear people say, "Oh, things are really going to change and be better in our new corporate headquarters." Eventually, the only things that change are the carpeting, furniture, and decor. When the components of integrated didactics are not considered, the same old thing is often the final outcome, and thus the move accomplishes very little except disillusionment.

In today's environment, to achieve high productivity and creativity, emphasis must be placed on the environment, the process, and the skills of people.

Staging of ability

A self-defeating fault committed by people who work on training and development programs is their failure to conduct a valid assessment of the levels of ability in the people who are going to be trained.

The very first action that we recommend is the staging of ability in order to understand where people are. This ensures that training programs you initiate will meet the needs of the pupils. A client once said to us, "Assess people first. Pick the winners. Then put time and money into training and developing the winners. Some people accidentally pick losers, throwing away a lot of time and money." We talked about this conversation after the session. At first, we were both bothered by this statement, and after we thought about it for awhile, we were *still* bothered by this statement, because we felt there was some truth to it.

A loser is a person who is not prepared to be successful in the job you are putting them in. You can give them assistance to get them prepared, but don't ruin the job by giving it to someone who can't do it. Identify the winners and the losers. This means determining aptitudes, qualities, or skills needed to do a task, and then matching them to potential characteristics. Send the losers to your competitor.

There was a dentist who wanted to raise the bar in his business practice, so, he set out to strengthen his foundation. He started by first identifying his customers. Winners were the A & B clients. These were the customers who needed or wanted a lot of work done and paid their bills promptly. Then he identified the C & D clients. These were the ones that were a pain to deal with, and who didn't have the means or the benefits to pay for his services. He figured that if he focused more on the A and B clients, that he would work less for higher profits.

So what did he do? He called up his competitor, the dentist next door! He kindly told his competitor that he wanted to play more golf and cut down on his own patient load. He offered his competitor some of his clients. The next door neighbor was delighted to have more clients. However, he got the C and D clients!

Right or wrong, good or bad, we need to begin the learning curve from the point where our students' needs and requirements are right now. Many trainers totally miss the mark, because they ignore this important principle.

Below are four "stages of ability." Once you understand them, you can use them to establish realistic programs for developing people.

- ➤ Wisdom
- ➤ Knowledge
- ➤ Awareness
- ➤ Ignorance

STAGING OF ABILITY

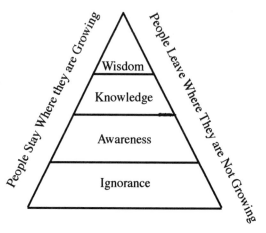

WHERE ARE YOUR PEOPLE?

STAGE	CAUSES	RESULTS
I. Ignorance •Not knowing that you don't know •Not stupid	A. No exposure B. No experience C. Ignoring things D. No training	A. Naivete B. Unrealistic thinking C. Being talked down to D. Indifference to growth
II. Awareness •Experience things •Feeling things •Not neurotic	A. Using all five senses B. Continuing to learn C. Having desire	A. Clean beginnings B. Exposure and learning C. Motivation
III. Knowledge •Having resources to meet your needs	A. The right environment, like a Team Center B. Resource-rich environments	A. Success in all five equities B. Achievement
IV. Wisdom •Wise beyond your age •Having accumulated learning with good sense	A. Practicing, which makes us better (but not perfect) B. Acceptance of life	A. Advancement B. Meditation C. Spiritual development

Let's look at each of these stages in greater detail. At the base of the pyramid is ignorance. Ignorance is unrealized potential, or a total lack of awareness concerning a problem. Ignorance should not be confused with lack of ability, or self-chosen stupidity. We don't believe that many people are actually stupid, but there are quite a few people who haven't had the opportunity or the right environment in which to develop themselves.

To advance to the second level of awareness, we must identify the areas where growth is needed by becoming aware of them. This must be achieved by honestly acknowledging faults, problems, and shortcomings. Once identified, you must then gain knowledge to determine how to overcome these gaps and shortcomings. It is here that you advance to the third level, knowledge. The learning organization has become a desired goal in many companies and homes.

Ability is our capacity to accomplish things. What we do is determined by what we are; what we are is determined by what we think; what we think is determined by what we learn; what we learn is determined by what we believe; and what you believe is determined by what we're exposed to and what we do with that exposure.

Finally, your efforts will lead to the fourth level, wisdom, where you will achieve more profound and philosophical understanding about yourself and the world in which we live. Wisdom is a stage that is surely needed in our culture today.

In your quest for kinetic knowledge, here is a quick reference to show you, step by step, how to powerfully climb through the four stages of ability:

The Staging of Ability

I. Ignorance—Being unaware of what you don't know; not stupidity

Causes	Results
A. No training	A. Unrealistic thinking—do not know
B. Ignoring Problems	B. Childish and naive behavior
C. No personal experience	C. Talking down to people
D. Lack of exposure	D. No desire to grow

II. Awareness—First hand experience, emotions, knowledge, and learning

Causes	Results
A. Thinking in all five senses.	A. New beginnings
B. Learning becomes a way of life	B. Knowledge and feelings
C. On the streetcar named desire	C. Motivated

III. Knowledge—Having the resources to meet needs or solve problems

Causes	Results
A. The right environment.	A. Raising the bar
B. High achievement	B. Resource-rich
C. Fulfillment of environment	C. Champions and models; objectives

IV. Wisdom—knowledge beyond your age

Causes	Results
A. Practicing, to become better	A. Advancement
B. Mediation	B. Acceptance of life

How to train people

"There are no bad dogs."
–Barbara Woodhouse, author and animal trainer

There are many ways we can develop and train people to achieve high performance. One of the unique teaching methods we discovered, the work-teach-model sequence, emerged from the Mae Carden method and the Socratic Teaching model.

Carden was an extraordinary educational theorist who pioneered brilliant teaching models that are used worldwide. Her methods were based on values that were both constructive and teachable.

The Socratic method is based on the law of causality, sometimes called the concept of "cause and effect." It requires the teacher to help students understand the effect by describing it to them and then explaining the causes behind it. This approach helps to reinforce the content for heightened learning.

Socrates (469-399 B.C.)

Socrates, the Greek philosopher from Athens, was considered to be one of the wisest men of all time. He left no writings of his own, but an understanding of his thoughts comes from the works of his most famous student—Plato. His method, known as Socratic dialogue, asked a series of questions from his students to get at the cause behind behavior. We currently refer to his training techniques as the Socratic method based on the Law of Causality, the concept of cause followed by effect. It requires a teacher to help the student understand the effect by describing it and explaining (teaching) the cause behind it.

Dr. Maria Montessori (1870-1952)

Dr. Montessori, the Italian educator and physician, was the inventor of the famed Montessori method for teaching small children. She developed didactic teaching materials, which the children themselves manipulate in order to learn. These materials are used around the world today by educators.

Dr. Montessori also designed and built children's furniture for use in her interactive classroom settings. Dr. Montessori was light years ahead of her time, promulgating advanced educational techniques at the turn of the twentieth century.

Mae Carden

Mae Carden, an author and teacher, founded a group of private schools which she named Carden Hall. Today, the Carden

Method curriculum created for grades one through 12 is used by more than 200 Carden-affiliated schools. Their success with students is legendary. Mike knew Miss Carden well and learned many training techniques from her that he used during his career as dean of Disney University, up to the present day.

Her teachings and influence on Mike led to the creation of the work-teach-model technique. Our favorite quote from Miss Carden came during one of her unforgettable workshops, "I am never after merely the right answer, but the mental process that provides the answer." This is truly thinking.

She, like Dr. Montessori, stressed the concept of cognitive reasoning—making certain that students understand the reasons behind the things learned. This also relates to the Socratic principle of cause and effect.

Seven training techniques

There are seven major training techniques that have proven effective over a long period of time. It is accurate to say that they have "stood the test of time," which we consider essential in qualifying for our own training. They're not our own, but they have been used extensively in our work with organizations around the world with outstanding results.

The seven training techniques have grown out of the teachings and philosophy of three intellectual giants in pedagogy: the Greek philosopher Socrates, Dr. Maria Montessori, and Mae Carden. Their ideas form the foundation for these proven methods and techniques that we'll study. We wish to acknowledge these teachers, give them credit for their contributions, and thank them for inspiring us in our work. The seven techniques are as follows:

1. Work-teach-model.
2. 1/3 essence, 2/3 details.
3. Teach and reteach.
4. Socratic method.
5. Immersion learning.
6. Autodidact.
7. Step up stages.

Training technique #1: Work-teach-model

The "work-teach-model" sequence is a technique that enables and reinforces learning by understanding an effect by experiencing it firsthand, then being taught the causes behind the experience (or the effect), and finally by observing a model performance of the task or concept to be learned.

> ➤ Work (experience, do the work, or demonstrate the task)—The effect.
> ➤ Teach (explain and answer questions)—The cause.
> ➤ Model (demonstrate best practices)—The example.

Example of work-teach-model

Domino's Pizza has used the work-teach-model technique in various locations. The first task that a new employee does during training is to stand next to the pizza maker at the table. They observe and actually hold the pizza and do the work with the pizza maker. This helps a new employee understand the effect and reinforce the learning experience.

This technique then advances to the second stage, which is teaching. This step can be held in a classroom discussion by asking the students what effects they observed, discussing them, and answering any questions that arise during the training. It's at this point that the teacher presents the cause, the "why" behind how things are being done. It is through understanding the effect, that curiosity arises about the cause, which creates interest and motivates students.

Finally, modeling of the best practices takes place to further reinforce the learning and set the example. Modeling can occur in three ways: in person, through a disciple, or through film or pictures. The best pizza maker, for example, demonstrates how to do the job better than the best.

You can have the person responsible for creating or establishing an idea demonstrate the example himself or herself. For example, we could have Walt Disney come in and talk about how he raised the bar in his organization. This would be an example of an in-person modeling session.

If that is impossible or impractical, the second way to present a model is to have someone who knew him, like Mike, talk about him to the students. These are called disciples. The third method is through audio visual support materials such as tapes, films, videos, overheads, power point, and so forth.

Take the training of a nurse, for surgery. We can ask the nurse to scrub in, stand next to the surgery table, observe, and perform tasks they can without causing any delays, interruption, or safety concerns. This is done in most teaching hospitals.

Now consider the same surgical nurse as she goes into the teaching amphitheater with her instructor after this experience in surgery. The teacher asks, "You've all been through the experience, do you have any questions?" This is referred to as pupil-driven learning. It is being driven on the level of the student's needs. Incidentally, these concepts can be applied to just about any profession or task.

After the teacher answers any questions, she says, "I'd like to present to you a model" and the students get to experience the procedure all over again, understanding what is behind it, and how it should be done. They witness the best example over again. This is personal modeling, which makes an indelible impression on students that often lasts a lifetime.

But often in modeling it is desirable to use all three techniques: the personal mode, disciples, and audio-visual. Why? It works as added reinforcement. A film is also effective because you can stop and look at a procedure that is being done, study it, and then go forward or backward as often as you like. You can pinpoint certain features and review them as often as needed. It's hard to do this when modeling is done only in person. You can't back up the operation and review it from the beginning in real time like you can on a videotape.

Another memorable illustration of the work-teach-model technique was with a nun whom we worked with who was the head of many Catholic hospitals. She was a wonderful woman who we liked very much. Mike had talked with her about these concepts and she said to him, "You know Mike, I bet we do not use any of these techniques in our hospitals. We have many nurses that do many procedures, which they have never had performed on them, consequently, they have little empathy." She said, "I think they need to experience the procedures they're doing to others as much as is possible."

This nun went to the endoscopic lab of her hospital and asked the nurses how many of them actually had ever experienced an endoscopic exam of the sigmoid colon? Of the group she asked, there were only five who had gone through the experience themselves. Her response was to change that immediately.

She requested that the entire group come to work early the next day because each nurse was going to have this exam, ensuring that they would experience it and understand how to do it. The nurses didn't respond enthusiastically.

The following day, the nurses came to work and got the exam. Having experienced it, they returned to the teaching center and the mother superior asked them if they had any questions. Every hand in the room went up and they all had questions. Once all of the questions were answered, someone asked if they could be given a demonstration. In this case they had a patient, a surgeon, and two nurses perform the procedure for the class. They observed it being done by the best practitioners. They videotaped the procedure, which enabled them to study specific parts of the exam and play them back as needed. Today, lawyers may object because of possible litigation.

However, the concept of work-teach-model is at the heart of excellent training. It helps people to become masters of their craft. Try it in places where you are responsible for the development of people's talents. It is one of the premier examples of how to raise the bar.

Training technique #2: 1/3 essence, 2/3 detail

The "one-thirds, two-thirds" method of training and developing people focuses on how time is utilized in teaching content in a course. One of the first things when planning a strategy to develop people is to prepare a timeline to follow. This timeline will denote how much time is allocated to each topic during the duration of training.

As a general rule, the most effective approach to use with people during initial training time is to preview for them what they will be learning throughout the course. This allows them to get the essence of the total course or curriculum from the beginning. On the training and development timeline, approximately one-third of the available training time is used to preview all subject matter to be learned. This is simply an overview of each course with no details discussed. The "essence time" allow pupils to set up the subjects in categories within their minds, which makes teaching easier.

The details are taught in the remaining 2/3 of the timeline. It is at this time teachers go through the work-teach-model sequence until the pupils succeed.

For example, when we helped create the GE Training Center for their locomotive division, we designed the work-teach-model method of learning right into the building. Students would first get a locomotive ride out on a test track in order to experience the ride. This was the first 1/3 of the learning sequence.

At a predetermined point, the locomotive would break down, and the class would have to determine why. They would go back to their classroom after this work-demonstrated experience and talk with the teacher about what went wrong. They would then observe the model approach for repairing the locomotive and improve upon it. Afterwards, they would see a film of previous students who learned to do it really well. This was the 2/3 portion of the learning sequence.

This learning center was designed so everybody was immersed in the total building. Its design included the work-teach-model technique and the 1/3 essence, 2/3 details principle. It is a model organizational approach to raising the bar in training.

Training technique #3: Teach and reteach

At the end of a training day, a student re-teaches the essence of what they just learned. It enables the teacher to do an accurate and realistic assessment of the students. The teacher can use the stages of ability pyramid to conduct this assessment, determining what, if anything, needs to be reviewed or altered in their curriculum or materials.

This technique is simple and straightforward: After learning from a teacher or from the work environment, one of the best ways to reinforce and expand upon the learning is to make the student the teacher. We have found it to be an exceptional approach that helps to insure the success in training efforts.

A leader who has successfully used many of these techniques in his leadership practices is Ken Dobler, vice president of new business development at Ethicon Endo-surgery, a Johnson & Johnson company. Ken has had a remarkable career in the development of outside sales training programs and techniques for Ethicon. He developed one of the finest sales representative organizations in the industry using "Think Out of the Box" tools, as well as the concept of teaching and reteaching.

The teach, reteach method was also used at the GE Learning Center. The center was designed to enable students to be divided into teams who attended the courses together. At the end of the training sessions (and noted on their training timeline), they would reserve an hour each day where the teams would create Displayed Thinking walls. They would create visuals and brief their instructors on what content they learned during the day. This enabled the instructors to know if students were grasping the content. It took the guesswork out of a realistic approach.

To get all "A" students, we can see how crucial the concept is of teach, re-teach. We know of schools that have used this approach in the past. For example, one outstanding teacher in the Pacific Northwest, Yvonne Hachiya, made her classroom into a Team Center. She used the techniques in teaching and working with her students and they would conduct the teach, reteach concept with her. She also employed the work-teach-model techniques so that her students really were immersed through the use of Displayed Thinking.

Training technique #4: The Socratic Method

The Socratic teaching method consists of the Law of Causality, based on the teachings of Socrates. It is used to present causes behind observed effects, Our awareness of this cause and effect relationship is called cognitive reasoning. For example, if we drop a rock off the top of a building it will fall to the ground (an effect). Physics teach us that the cause behind this effect is gravitational force.

Dr. Montessori stressed the importance of students' understanding the cause behind various actions. We often arrive at the cause by asking the fundamental question of why something is the way it is, which eventually leads us to a conclusion.

Teaching often focuses entirely on the task in order to get people working quietly, omitting the step of getting at the cause and weakening the results. We have learned that even the simplest task will be done better when people understand the reason behind it.

Training technique #5: Immersion learning

Immersion learning is what it sounds like: total immersion in a subject. "Up to our ears" is a description of what immersion is like for the student. Living and breathing our studies, is often another way of saying it. The technique of immersion learning calls for total involvement and commitment on behalf of the students and teachers. In other words, we go all the way in order to ensure the maximum results in our training.

The education and qualification of doctors in the medical profession is one of the best examples of immersion learning that everyone is familiar within the United States. There is a combination of classroom teaching, on the job experience, practice, cadaver dissection, mentoring and testing, and so forth.

Training technique #6: The autodidactic

Autodidactic teaching is the practice of teaching oneself or being engaged in self-study. Didactic means to primarily instruct or teach. (Dr. Montessori pioneered in the invention of didactic teaching materials, meaning, materials created exclusively for the purpose of teaching.) Dr. Montessori's didactic teaching materials are aids to being an autodidact.

Ideally, part of all training should consist of lessons that are autodidactic, based on independent study. At the rate knowledge proliferates today, it is essential for everyone to be involved in continuing education and self-improvement. This love of learning is now a requirement for continued success in every profession. The habits of being autodidactic are the descriptions leading to personal development and personal survival today.

Training technique #7: Step-up stages

Placing and timing have long been recognized as important issues in the learning process. There is a time to crawl and there is a time to walk. In fact, as mentioned, behaviorists today caution parents from pushing children too fast through the crawling stage of development, because studies indicate that this can be severely damaging.

Step up stages plan for the progressive learning of steps or phases an individual goes through to master a task or skill. Students gain confidence as they successfully complete one phase and then move on to another phase.

Learning becomes cumulative, each part resting on a previous part until we are prepared. The "prepared mind" concept is one of the key practices to raise the bar. (Blaise Pascal, the 17th century French scientist and philosopher, was one of the first to observe that breakthroughs and innovations come from the "Prepared Mind.")

Tips on training failures

The well-intentioned admonition to "keep trying" doesn't always work on the firing line. We can beat our heads against the wall without any tangible results for only so long. This is not to say that we should give up easily or fail at being tenacious in our attempts to succeed. However, there comes a time when we must face the fact that our methods are failing.

We have observed common training failures in our experiences that have resulted in these tips for you to consider in evaluating your progress.

1. Not pinpointing the major cause of failure.

Students' learning habits.

Teachers' skills.

Poor environment.

Tasks are unclear.

Materials poor or inferior plans.

2. Efforts spoiled by realities in business, work, or home.

Poor managers and leaders.

Unfair practices, politics, nepotism, scheduling.

Excessive control, authoritarianism, prejudices, attitudes.

3. Algorithmic vs. heuristic methods.

Step by step rigid procedures vs. experimental procedures.

4. Unseen factors at work.

Fatigue of students and/or teachers, overworked, unrealistic expectations, faulty equipment, fuzzy goals, favoritism, mood swings, and so forth.

5. Skipping steps/taking short cuts.

Eliminating the crawl before the walk, reducing practice time, doing before qualifying.

6. Ignoring the teaching moment.

The teaching moment, as described by Dr. Montessori, is that time when the student is ready to learn, usually corresponding with the moment of maximum need.

7. Doing steps incorrectly.

Failure is often the result of doing a task or a procedure incorrectly in the teaching mode.

8. Lack of credibility.

Teachers who lack credibility with their students often demotivate them.

9. Not using proven learning tools.

Not using the seven training techniques discussed here.

10. Too much material presented in a given time.

Students cannot process large chunks of information.

Principles for raising the bar: Strategy #4

✓ Develop a method to evaluate potential.

✓ Be sure creativity is ethically applied.

✓ Consider the place, the people, and the product.

✓ Use proven training techniques.

✓ Understand and avoid the causes of training failures.

✓ Have an organizational development and leadership program.

✓ Identify pathfinders.

✓ Develop pathfinders.

(For further information, see our *Developing People* audio program.)

Personal applications

The music box

When Vanessa Vance was only a few months old she was like any other baby. Around midnight, she sent out the unmistakable signal that she was ready for her bottle. Mike lifted her out of the bassinet, cradling her body in his arms. The baby stopped crying, and the two lay silently on the floor for a few minutes.

On the floor next to them was a very small music box. It was enclosed in a glass dome that revealed a tiny ballerina dressed in pink. Mike wanted to teach Vanessa the principles for starting the music box.

Mike watched as Vanessa reached out with one hand toward the music box. Perhaps she was ready to learn, even with the warm bottle of milk standing by. Dr. Montessori wrote of the "teaching moment," the moment when there is motivation to learn.

Mike decided that a demonstration would be the best teaching method in this situation. He placed the box in the palm of his hand, holding it close to Vanessa's face. Both of their noses touched the sides of the glass enclosure; there was an on-off lever about an inch in length on the side of the box. Mike said, "I'm going to start the music box." He then placed his fingers on the lever, gave it a tug, heard a click, and listened as the music began to play and the dancer began to dance. Vanessa beamed.

Mike repeated the demonstration three times and noticed that the smile got brighter each time. Mike decided Vanessa was ready, she was at a teaching moment. He helped her through the steps required to start the music. He placed her index finger and thumb on the lever with his fingers on top of them. He said, "Let's start the music. I'll tug at the lever." Together, they started the music box; again it clicked, and the music began to play and the dancer began to dance. They repeated this assisted exercise three times; each time Vanessa became more excited.

She was now reaching, trying to move the lever herself. Mike held the box for her and placed her fingers on the lever. He said, "Vanessa, start the music box." She smiled and began to pull at the lever. She gave it several tugs—and suddenly it clicked. The music played. The dancer danced. Vanessa was thrilled. She repeated the process, with Mike placing her fingers on the lever over and over again.

Mike will never forget the experience of watching Vanessa as he took the music box out of his hand and placed it in her palm. Her small hand trembled; no doubt the music box looked enormous to her. Mike watched as she tugged at the lever, all by herself this time. She kept at it until it clicked, the music played, and the dancer danced.

She squealed in joy, as if to say, "I did that!" The teaching moment was fulfilled.

Vanessa experienced both the understanding of cause and effect, as well as the satisfaction of doing something herself. The process of self-esteem had begun to unfold.

"Everyone is a genius at least once a year—a real genius has his original ideas closer together." –G.C. Lichtenberg

Eureka!

Imagine that a cloud covering the lens of one eye is gradually obstructing vision. Time to face reality, Mike Vance. You have to do something about your vision. You have a cataract.

Suddenly, there are frightening images of surgery, hospitals, thick glasses, a long period of recovery, or even blindness. Or perhaps the initial reaction is simple denial. Before you know it, it's nearly impossible to drive at night. You can't see because the headlights from other cars turn everything else into a hazy white blur.

We decided to think about this dilemma by asking some fundamental questions: What are the state of the art technology and procedures today in cataract surgery? Who is the best cataract surgeon in the world? Diane immediately began to research this issue to locate the better than the best of cataract surgeons. She found it necessary to search our contacts, our friends, doctors we knew, and our clients. We got a hot lead from our friends at the General Electric medical division.

Mike knew the GE guys would know where the state of the art in cataract surgery was—this is, after all, one of their fields of expertise. One of their leaders told us to contact Dr. Stephen Trokel in New York City. Dr. Trokel had pioneered the use of the Yag laser in a new procedure in cataract surgery. Coincidentally, Diane read an article in *Time* Magazine about the revolutionary applications in cataract surgery being made with the Yag laser by Dr. Trokel.

At the time, we were working in Manhattan on a project for Avon Products. Diane telephoned Dr. Trokel and he said to come on over to his office, which we proceeded to do that afternoon.

Dr. Trokel was a fascinating man who got right to the point after we walked into his office. He asked what we were looking for. We said, "We're looking for the state of the art cataract surgeon in the entire world. Do you know who it is and where that person might be?"

He chuckled at both of us saying, "You're the creative thinkers. You tell me, where would this surgeon be located?"

"Where the cataracts are!" Mike responded.

"Right," he laughed back. "He's where there are more cataracts per square inch than any other place in the world. Near your home, Mike."

"Florida!" we both said simultaneously.

"Your man is Dr. James P. Giles in New Port Richey, Florida. He is the very best cataract surgeon living. He does more procedures than anyone else and is ahead of the pack. He founded the St. Luke's Eye Center and pioneered an amazing surgical procedure. He leaves your original lens intact, removing only the ripe cataract with fica emulsification in order to cut down on trauma and shorten the healing time. If it clouds up again, which rarely happens, the Yag Laser is used to zap it. If you want to meet Dr. Giles, let me call him right now and set up an appointment."

Thus began an exciting adventure for us. We met Dr. James P. Giles, a great surgeon, but more importantly, a great person dedicated to unsurpassed excellence. He raised the bar to the very highest notch in the medical profession. He actually took an interest in and cared about his patients.

We want to describe for you what we saw the first time we visited St. Luke's:

At approximately 6:30 in the morning, there were two lines of about 30 people standing outside of the entrance doors into the clinic. Half of the people had a patch covering one of their eyes, indicating they had the implant procedure the day before. The other half of the people, who all had the heebie-jeebies, were going to go through the procedure that morning.

Amazingly, the "patches" were reassuring the "non-patch" wearers. They were naturally nervous and frightened about what was ahead for them. But those "patch people" just looked at them and kept remarking that, "Today is going to be the most beautiful day of your life!" How could having eye surgery be considered a beautiful day?

What we witnessed following this introduction in the street was nothing short of spectacular in every way. It was the best example of customer service and treating people with respect and dignity that we have ever seen anywhere. Mike knew that Walt Disney himself would have sent up 10 flares of approval into the Florida skies.

A woman who didn't act like a receptionist in any way greeted patients again inside the reception area. She acted like their friend immediately by her exceptional people skills, making them feel like people instead of patients. She too said, "This is going to be the most beautiful day of your life!"

Everyone was seated in a beautiful setting that seemed more like a living room than a holding area for surgery patients. The lounge was simple, but filled with little touches that made everyone feel at ease and welcomed. There was information on the upcoming surgery including a large screen video featuring Dr. Giles explaining their day and the procedure to the waiting patients. There were candles, religious objects, and even stained glass windows. The feeling was perfect.

Each person went through a number of stations in preparation for their time in the operating room. We watched many people go through each step. They were handled with gentleness and caring by an obviously dedicated team that Dr. Giles had trained.

The surgery itself did not take long. Dr. Giles touched people on the shoulder or squeezed their hands as he began. He said, "the next time I touch your shoulder, we will be finished."

The patient is handed a fresh flower at the conclusion of the surgery, establishing an even deeper rapport with the doctor.

(Having something nice to smell and touch doesn't hurt morale, either.) We can't describe the feeling that exists within this environment. It is simply unparalleled.

Dr. Giles is not only an impressive physician. Dr. Giles has been a competitive triathlete and he participates in various triathlons. He told us one afternoon what caused him to achieve his breakthrough cataract procedures, a discovery that raised the bar in his profession even higher.

One day he was riding his bicycle from his home to the St. Luke's Eye Center. As he was leaving his driveway his bicycle tire accidentally ran over a garden hose with a portable sprinkler attached to it for watering a portion of his grass. He noticed that the pressure from the tire on the hose caused the sprinkler to stop. Eureka!

He had made a breakthrough by association. He envisioned a way to insert a lens during cataract surgery without using any stitches to hold it in place. He reasoned that the pressure within the eye would hold the lens in place without stitches. He was right. His procedure was simplified even more, leading to easier and shorter recoveries.

This breakthrough was stimulated by the simple act of running over a garden hose with a bicycle. Stitchless cataract surgery was born. Thousands of people have benefited from the innovations of Dr. Giles and his remarkable staff.

The Creative Thinking Association of America presented Dr. Giles with one of their highest awards for achievement—The National Recognition Award. There isn't enough praise possible for the exemplary work of St. Luke's Eye Center and this exceptional medical missionary, Dr. James Giles.

We need breakthroughs

It's important to pin down and identify where the breakthroughs are being created in our organizations. People claim to be busy working day in and day out, stuck in a routine of reporting endlessly on what they've done, what they are doing, or what they will be doing. All this reporting leaves little time to work on breakthrough ideas and solutions. We hear this excuse every day from people claiming they have no time for creative thinking. Everyone is always "too busy." What they should be saying is that they want to use time more efficiently, in order to commit the effort and energy necessary to help ensure breakthroughs in the future. The desire and motivation are usually there in individuals and organizations, a creative process that is understood and used. Failure to devote time to creative thinking is extremely shortsighted and ultimately produces an absence of innovation, which jeopardizes a business.

There are currently indicators that this is taking place in our companies on a large scale as witnessed by the lack of originality in new products. There has been a steady decline in the quality of patents issued and applied for in the United States Patent Office in recent years, even though we've experienced many technical innovations. This is a tragic state of affairs. We're missing out on the challenge that was left to future generations by Thomas Edison, who said, "Create something new for us."

There is still time to accept his challenge! There are many critical needs, opportunities, and problems that cry out for breakthrough solutions—the kind that require competence, dedication, and passion to develop. We need "break out of the box" thinkers to turn up the heat. Many problems need fixing or improving in today's society: Education in pace with technology, curing the right disease when we're in the hospital, reducing the number of people who's careers don't last, creating more jobs, spending tax revenue on important issues, improving television programming to raise people's tastes—the list goes on forever. These are only some of the exciting opportunities for everyone to improve society by beginning a cultural renaissance. It is the time for revival, rebirth, reinventing, and reestablishing ourselves as motivated and creative people.

When we work with organizations that are striving for breakthroughs, we've discovered that key people within these organizations commit early to support a creative thinking process. They don't coast along on what they have, but reach out with results that keep new product ideas flowing in the pipeline. Don't wait until the pipeline dries up before engaging in creative thinking—it's often too late. Plan social events and celebrations regularly to light people's fires! As the rock music group sings, "Come on baby light my fire!"

Smart people don't fall into the trap of assuming that creative thinking will take care of itself without leadership. Smart people don't make the huge mistake of believing they're so good, too successful, and so smart that they don't need to actively nurture creative thinking in order to develop breakthrough ideas and solutions. They actually read the books they buy instead of displaying them on coffee tables. It's time to fill the intellectual vacuum.

Achieving big breakthroughs require that we have a place to "fish" for record-breaking "trophy ideas." Therefore, we again recommend that you create a Team Center, a creative environment that provides resources for individuals and teams to promote creativity, teamwork and innovation. It's essential to establish "The Place" which we will emphasize over and over.

Solutions are only temporary events

We also need a reliable method for catching the trophy fish or big ideas. We all know that good ideas just don't happen, smart thinking is no accident, that to catch the really big, trophy fish requires exceptional skills along with unique tools and methods. What are the tools and techniques you'll employ? What kind of fishing rod will you use? What kind of lures or hooks will you put in your tackle box? We recommend our "Think out of the Box" techniques along with our Displayed Thinking system, because they have proven to help people achieve breakthrough solutions. We live to help someone over the bar of mediocrity. One of the most exciting accomplishments in the world, as leaders or parents, is watching someone become something extraordinary. What follows are important points to keep in mind.

Recognize the best fishermen

Once we hook up by getting a big idea on the line, who makes the value judgment that it's not just another good idea but a breakthrough solution? Who tests out the idea to see if it will fly? And who will implement it? Are your "fishermen" given recognition and appropriately rewarded for catching their "big idea"? People stop fishing when no one says to them, "What a great idea you caught! Here's a reward. Go do it again!" Fishermen have to show you their lines filled with fish; idea fishers will proudly hold up for you to admire their lines full of creative ideas.

Don't solve this year's problems with last year's solutions

Catching the next big fish gets harder and harder because we raise our standards and expectations. Success and fame are really fleeting things; one solution is never enough. We need tools, techniques, and methods to keep the solutions and the breakthroughs coming. This is called a creative thinking process.

In our seminars and project development work, we often run into people who try to solve this year's problems with last year's solutions. This is a major fault, but it's actually easy to understand why this happens so often. Last year's solutions sometimes work well. But sometimes they don't, and when they don't, you must commit yourselves to learning from them to improve tomorrow. This requires that you don't brush things under the table or rationalize and compromise your values just to make things turn out right.

To innovate and to move ahead, you need to establish a habit for trying out new approaches. This is not done by resting on your past accomplishments. You have to be willing to take risks and challenge yourself by asking the question, "What else could work even better than what I am doing?" You need a healthy addiction that compels you through dedication to be experimental. Isn't it strange how easily people get addicted to drinking, drugs, gambling, and sex. Perhaps we need treatment centers for the addiction to conformity and non-creative thinking as well! (Our seminars and products are meant to provide an effective cure to this illness!)

Companies often take a product that is a top performer because of its uniqueness in concept and design, then ride with it until it dies. We know of several companies with large research and development budgets that have a disturbing problem; they invest millions of dollars in research for new products, but nothing new ever seems to come out the other end! It's like taking a herd of cattle, putting them through a meat grinder, and one meatball falls out. They still have the old patents or products, but no real breakthroughs have evolved. They keep solving this year's problems with last year's solutions, a recipe of market complacency that can wipe you out. Eventually, even a robust market will begin to soften if there's no innovation, or no attempt to make products better!

Smart leaders don't wait until their market position collapses. They get out there and test new stuff! Try some new things. Replace talk with action. Do it! Take on new initiatives! Experiment.

Of course, it makes sense to try the new with incremental steps, in order to prevent the undertaking from becoming a shock, causing trauma to the organization. In spite of this, we must constantly challenge ourselves to create and to innovate. We must never be content with our credentials from past achievements. Past successes will not bear the weight of increasing competition. At some point, copyrights, trademarks, and patents will expire, disappear, or be stolen, diminishing the value of the company. They are not permanent solutions! In today's fast moving world, they must be constantly refreshed with new concepts, new ideas, new products, and new innovations.

Think like God

Several years ago, Mike was asked to speak at the American Institute of Architects convention in Los Angeles, and he talked about Wright's, Disney's, and Fuller's concepts of divinity and its effect on their design. Some people believe that Wright thought he was God, Walt Disney knew he was not God, and Buckminster Fuller said he knew God! Each of their points of view about God, of finding ways to think like God, influenced the work of these three geniuses.

We were first attracted to this idea when we heard the same expression from two of our favorite people at two separate times. Frank Lloyd Wright, when he would sit at a drafting table with his students, would ponder on how God would design a project. Because Wright was thinking about how the Creator would do it, he was able to tap into the beauty of nature in many of his remarkable structures. The results of this approach were so striking that, if you were an atheist, you'd probably be tempted to pretend that you believed in God for a moment, just so you could have a chance of getting work done at that level!

Walt Disney had a profound understanding and respect for what the talents of a team could add to an enterprise because he knew he couldn't do every task it takes to make a memorable motion picture like *Snow White and the Seven Dwarfs* or *Fantasia*. It takes a team to accomplish tasks on this scale. Walt believed there was a little of God in each of us. He assumed that when we think like God, we're actually acknowledging the God within us. He wanted to encourage that divinity within to come out, so the rest of the world could benefit. This is one of the reasons why he emphasized the importance of developing others and ourselves.

Fuller both saw and understood the spiritual side of the universe in a very profound way. We both felt honored knowing this extraordinary man who once observed that "the major resources are already created because we live in a world of operating general principles that are worthy of emulation." By this, he meant that we could find reliable principles in the universe for creative living and fulfillment. We can adapt or utilize them if we are devoted to learning.

For Fuller, God was the "universal designer" that was capable of guiding and inspiring profound work. What is God for you? Think like God, and see what happens.

The Creative Zone

The Creative Zone is a place where the maximum creativity is achieved. Runners call this zone their endorphin high. One doesn't always stay in this zone. We want to discuss how you get into the zone and how can you increase your frequency of getting into the Creative Zone so that you raise the baseline and the bar.

There are three ways to tap into the creativity that exists everywhere. They are:

1. Study the General Principles as seen within nature and the universe. (Frank Lloyd Wright, Buckminster Fuller, and Thomas Edison all agreed that everything they ever designed or invented appeared in nature).
2. Within you is a Creative Muscle just waiting to be exercised and stimulated.
3. Team with others to add their talents and skills to reach the Creative Zone.

Philosophical entry into the Creative Zone

We all seek to enter the Creative Zone when we are confronted with a challenge of almost any kind or intensity. There seems to be an innate urge within each person to find some special place or to enter a pure state of mind that will produce insight by revealing an outstanding solution.

Shangri-La, that idyllic hide away, beckons to us all in different ways:

➢ Saints seek a revelation in the zone through abstinence.
➢ Sinners seek reformation in the zone through prayer.
➢ Inventors seek ideas in the zone through exploration.
➢ Athletes seek mastery in the zone through inner focus.
➢ Leaders seek guidance in the zone through deep thought.
➢ Entrepreneurs seek advantage in the zone through the creative process.
➢ Parents seek wisdom in the zone through dedication.

Philosophic entry to the Creative Zone means a calm temperament and composure in judgment. Often in the heat of battle, at the height of competition, at the most intense and critical moments, at the peak of frustration, at the point of overwhelming need—it is time to withdrawal from the fray by entering into the Creative Zone.

There is also an urge during our "highs" and "lows" for returning to homeostasis. The Creative Zone helps us to reestablish our equilibrium on a higher plane. Models and examples show us doorways leading into the zone.

Meditation/cogitation/levitation

During a press interview with the great American theoretical physicist, Albert Einstein, he was asked what inspired him and what drove him to continue his quest for knowledge. As a physicist, he used the metaphor of a giant clock to represent the universe.

He said that the giant clock had never been opened for a first hand look inside because scientists couldn't pry the back off to get a good look. The hands on the clock are moving and scientists could speculate on how the inner mechanics worked. Reporters asked if he believed anyone would ever get the back off this metaphorical clock to postulate an accurate unified theory. He replied that he didn't think it would ever happen.

They pressed him further for an explanation by asking him why he continued searching and looking if he knew it was futile. He replied, "It's the ticking. It's the ticking inside the clock that we hear which keeps us thinking. You have to hear the ticking."

For Einstein, the zone was entered via the use of a metaphor and the sound of ticking. Cogitation is the deep thinking that takes us to places of discovery and insight.

Thomas Edison practiced meditation to enter the zone, which was told to us by his personal friend, Jim Newton, author of *Uncommon Friends*. Everyday before working in his Fort Myers, Florida, lab he would go fishing out on the end of his long dock. You can still visit his home in Fort Myers and take a walk on that same dock where he meditated daily. He wore an old overcoat, a hat and sat on a bench at the very end of the dock.

His fishing pole was held carefully to avoid any unnecessary movement that might scare away the fish. Alas, we learned from Jim Newton that there was no hook or bait on the end of his line. Edison once remarked that without a hook he was wasn't disturbed by either fish or man. He found that nobody bothered him when he was out fishing, making it the perfect time for meditation. He called it "cosmic fishing for big ideas."

For Edison the zone was entered via cosmic fishing all alone on a dock without a hook or bait. It was meditation in the quietness and serenity of a Florida morning that caused him to catch some of the biggest ideas of the 20th century.

Buckmister Fuller practiced a kind of "levitation" to enter the zone, which he told us about one evening at dinner. We asked Bucky how he remained creative and active even in his 80s. How did he enter the Creative Zone? What exactly did he do to achieve it?

He said, "I still have the hobby horse that I rode as a child. I keep making discoveries by continuing to ride that horse even as an adult. It causes my perspective to increase by sitting on the horse as a big person, but remembering and feeling what it was like as a child. It caused me to levitate between my past, the present, and the future. I often felt as if I was suspended six inches above the horse looking down. My mind became receptive through perspective."

For Fuller the zone was entered via levitating above his childhood hobbyhorse. Mental levitation takes us above the ordinary into a place of clear vision and perspective.

Whenever she can, Diane enters the zone by early morning walks on Florida's Gulf Coast beaches. She listens to music on her Walkman and breathes in the fresh salty air. Mike enters the zone by what he calls "themed sleeping." He thinks of something that he wants to create as he falls asleep. During the night, he will awaken and make notes on what he dreamed.

Our address is on the book jacket; please write to us and share the ways you enter the Creative Zone.

In the zone

As you learn to enter the zone more often you will discover that it is a temporary event. Athletes don't run at a maximum speed for long. They don't sprint forever through the entire race. A racehorse does not run at top speed for the whole race but it is "let out" in order to pass. Put aside a routine time when you enter the zone. Pick a place that enables you to enter the zone. Entering the Creative Zone brings you to a higher place, thus raising the bar.

Ideation techniques to make breakthroughs

Ideation techniques are principles that can lead to original thinking and exciting new solutions. For more detailed information on Ideation Techniques, please refer to Chapter Eight of our book *Think Out Of The Box*. What follows is a summary of some of the major ideas from that chapter. They have proven to be powerful. Utilize the Displayed Thinking system to apply these ideation techniques both personally and professionally. We teach various ideation techniques in our seminars. What follows are a few proven hints to help you raise the bar!

Develop your unique factor

Unique factors are what differentiates one thing from another. If you have a unique factor, people will want to take advantage of what you have to offer, and they will come to you. You're the only person who offers it! The unique factor is often the cause for patents, copyrights, and trademarks.

One of the most important parts of raising the bar is making a commitment to develop a unique factor within your business. The more you act like yourself, the less you are like anyone else, which alone gives you a unique factor. A great example of a unique factor is the Coca-Cola Company. It has a unique factor, which is a proprietary formula for producing a unique cola drink. Nobody else has the exact combination of flavors. In order to get Coca-Cola's distinct taste—Coca-Cola's unique factor—you have to buy its product!

Barbra Streisand's voice is like no other. Her talented voice is her unique factor. For those of us who can only hope to hum as well as Barbra, unique factors for us can be as simple as having the best recipe in the neighborhood for chocolate chip cookies, or having the ability to put on the best themed holiday parties.

Constantly "plus"

One way to achieve a breakthrough solution is to "plus" whatever is currently unique to you, and not available anywhere else. Improving and expanding what you currently offer to others can enhance your unique factor. For example, the common pencil was plused by adding an eraser to the other end. Likewise the corkscrew was improved by adding a bottle opener to it.

Another excellent example of plusing is what Procter & Gamble and Kimberly Clark do with their brands of disposable diapers. They're always adding special design features to their products. Follow their lead by using the technique of plusing a reality in your world. Make a point of adding innovation and creativity to the unique factor in your products.

An interesting illustration of plusing is practiced by a children's dentist in Ohio with whom we've had the pleasure of working with. This dentist took plusing to a whole new level in his young customers' experience. He tried to analyze his dental office through the eyes of a child in order to create a less threatening environment for them. When entering the office, a child experienced child-sized furniture and a receptionist window that was built at the child's eye level. Once inside, the child was guided down halls that were lined with pictures of the dentists and hygienists on staff. Fun facts about each person were placed under their photos. The children were encouraged to look at the photos and select the friendly faces that would work on them. Every room that a child entered—from x-rays to teeth cleaning—was decorated around a theme, such as kite flying, underwater aquarium, sports, and so forth. As a grand finale to their experience, when each child prepared to leave, they were asked if they would like an autographed picture of their dentist to hang up at home! This dentist in Ohio built one of the largest children's practices in the United States by utilizing the art of plusing his environment.

Another example is McDonald's Restaurant. They are constantly plusing their format. McDonald's started out as just a hamburger and fries restaurant. Then they plused their format and added other products, as well as a dining area. Then, they added more items to the menu. They added a drive-through pick up window. Today some restaurants have playgrounds for kids to play in. They are continually plusing their business.

Romance your ideas

Another technique to develop break out of the box solutions is to romance your ideas. Make them unique and bigger than life by lifting them up to a higher plane of excellence.

Walt Disney used this concept for the benefit of everyone by blowing new life into the old-time amusement. Walt essentially invented a theme park that brings out the child in young and old alike. Before Walt, the typical amusement park had a shady reputation for theft and the mistreatment of children. They were dismal places compared to today's elaborate and well-run parks.

Romancing often requires bringing fantasy into life. We previously worked with a bookstore owner in the midwest who utilized this technique to create fantasy in his bookstore and to catch people's attention. This bookstore, which was located in a mall adjacent to a hotel, wasn't selling enough books to make ends meet. Fearful that he was going to lose his business, the owner asked us to help with his employees to create a unique bookstore. Our challenge was to make it an attraction that would make people want to visit it, even if they weren't interested in buying books.

First, we made design changes to the physical layout of the store. We added the romance by making it more hospitable and user-friendly. When a customer walked into the bookstore from the mall, their eyes were drawn immediately to two wing chairs that were placed on an Oriental rug. These were placed in the center of the entrance with lights shining on them, and a candle burning on an end table. Two employees were dressed in costume with their hair swept atop of their head and each were called "Madame Librarian." Music from *The Music Man* played in the background.

Shoppers would hear this music and see the librarians sitting in the chairs (one even held a cat) with stacks of books surrounding them. Down each book aisle were places where you could sit down, look at a book, and enjoy a cup of coffee.

Customers were entranced by the bookstore. Let's take a look at a typical customer's experience: A man took a walk through the mall, and what do you think caught his eye? Madame Librarian surrounded by books, sitting in a wing chair stroking her cat. She then invited him to come in, sit down, and have a cup of coffee. She asked him, as if it was built into a script, "Are you a golfer?" The man responded that he was. She inquired, "How do you like this new book on Arnold Palmer, it just came out?" as she handed it to him. Well this gentleman was "hooked" by her friendliness. He wasn't thinking about books when he walked in the mall, yet he walked out of the bookstore with a sack full of books.

He got caught up in the fantasy, environment, and uniqueness of it all. The bar of bookstores was raised. The store became a success and helped create the trend we see in many bookstores today.

Creativity: Making the new from the old

We wrote in Strategy Number Two that part of the MICORBS process involves bringing seemingly unrelated issues together, in order to bring about a breakthrough. We do this by facilitating a "Synapse Session" using the Displayed Thinking process in order to come up with novel combinations using forced relationships and metaphoric thought.

We've been discussing various ideation techniques, such as romancing, plusing, and creating a unique factor. However, sometimes we need to make our products or ideas more interesting and appealing. This is where rearranging the old in a new way comes into play. There is nothing worse than a product with no appeal. Such a product is boring, lacks luster, and isn't inviting to the consumer.

Lawry's Prime Rib restaurant in Los Angeles is a well-known example of rearranging the old in a new way. The founders and owners, the Van de Camps and Lawrence Frank, wanted to make their restaurants stand out from all others. To illustrate their differences, Richard Frank appeared on Mike's television program in Los Angeles and described some of their unique features. One restaurant was designed around a magnificent wine cellar that could be reserved for small private parties. In another location, they thought it would be interesting if they changed the presentation of the meal by having the salad served last instead of first, as is the custom in most countries outside the United States. They also tossed their customers' salad right at their tables, rather than in the kitchen. Later, they manufactured their own brand of salad dressings and seasonings called "Lawry's."

Lawry's Prime Rib created the new by truly rearranging the old in a new way. They developed their restaurant and product uniquely including the preparation and the setting.

Sensanation: Thinking in all 5 senses

Sensanation is learning to think in all five senses—sight, sound, taste, touch and smell. It extends thinking beyond the visual or the forming of images called imagination.

One form of sensanation is the utilization of sound, primarily music, to stimulate the thinking mood, arouse emotions, and add spirit to the mise-en-scene. It is an effective technique to develop out of the box solutions.

The Mozart Effect

"Music will make you smarter."
–Don Campbell, National Music Association Convention

The Mozart Effect is the phenomenon where listening to music—especially the great classical works of Wolfgang Amadeus Mozart—improves one's IQ immediately after hearing it. It has been said that music can actually increase your IQ by as much as 30 percent. According to a study published in Don Campbell's' compelling work, *The Mozart Effect* (Avon Books), students who sing or play a musical instrument score up to 10 to 30 points higher on SATs than the national average. We recommend his book highly. It is a must read for aspiring and experienced creative thinkers.

Mike recently spoke to the National Music Association Convention in the Los Angeles Convention Center, where along one side of the building hung a huge banner claiming that "Music Will Make You Smarter."

These seemingly far-out claims piqued our interest to search further into the truth of this matter. Our appetites were even further whetted when *USA Today* reported the discovery in an article featured several years ago. Concurrently, the NBC television network ran an hour-long special report entitled "The Incredible Brain" in which the Mozart Effect was examined and authenticated by investigators.

There is a growing body of data validating the efficacy of the Mozart Effect for enhancing and stimulating creativity. But while there exists considerable important findings about the Mozart Effect, there is still considerable debate about how much listening to Mozart will actually raise your intelligence. Regardless of the debate, the findings show that it does happen, and the Mozart Effect can be demonstrated when comparing musical with non-musical environments.

We recently had this point dramatically reinforced when we were invited to a Mozart Symphony in Cleveland, Ohio, as the guests of Richard Morrison, president and CEO of The Molded Fiberglass Companies. It was a spectacular evening. Mozart's career, of course, remains staggering. This remarkable prodigy was composing music at age five and had a large body of work by age 13. As a composer he was without equal, leaving us with a rich legacy of beautiful sound to be appreciated and enjoyed. He raised the bar very high. And now there is evidence that listening to the music of such genius will further improve our intellectual capacity.

Try it! Play a specially selected Mozart composition in your Team Center to stimulate your creative juices. We're not saying that we should all become musicologists, but it's valuable to make time for music appreciation and IQ-lifting.

A primary purpose of music is to stimulate our emotions, our passions, and our spirit, establishing a mood and an atmosphere. Motion picture directors know that the right musical score can help make a film unforgettable. We expect a marching band in a parade, a romantic ballad in a love story, an abrasive electronic organ at a hockey game, carols at Christmas, and hymns at Easter. Do you remember the use of Ravel's Bolero in the motion picture comedy *10* featuring Bo Derek? It is simple: The music was unforgettable!

Music should be important to our lives. It is energy for the mind. Therefore, we'd like to make these suggestions to you:

1. If you're not already doing so, begin listening to the music of Mozart. Try for the effect. It can help you to increase your creativity and raise your IQ.
2. If you're not already playing a musical instrument, begin by learning how to play piano. Then, teach your children. The piano is very easy to learn at the start. A piano is very basic in music because learning a keyboard instrument introduces students to many musical terms.
3. If you're not already singing, buy a karioke machine for your Team Center or Kitchen for the Mind and begin developing your voice. We have found in our home that a karioke machine gets a considerable amount of use. It helps children and adults develop their voice by singing along. Singing gives us a wonderful pastime and builds confidence in your skills.

If you're already doing these musical activities, we urge you to challenge others to give them a try. The Mozart Effect, piano lessons and singing will all enrich your life. So will the act of putting words and thoughts to music!

A lusty appetite: Test and try nearly everything!

"Go for it!" We had the exciting opportunity of working on concepts for a new Mexican restaurant format at Brinker International Restaurant Company. Every night for nearly a month we dined out at different restaurants in town and ordered just about one of everything on the menu in order to come up with unique factors and differentiators. We were looking for a synaptic connection between the various parts of a restaurant to create a *new* format. These visitations were our homework and research. We had the appetite for knowledge because Norman Brinker wanted ideas for a Mexican format that would be used in his plans for a new chain of restaurants. It was a very successful project with numerous features that later became part of Chili's and Macaroni Grill. What we learned from all the testing and trying ideas out was the need for a Mexican dish that wasn't being used by others. The fajita was improved, and romanced. The result? A huge increase in popularity.

The Greek Ideation Techniques

The following ideation techniques were used to distinguish some different types of motivational factors. These factors are often considered effective mapping strategies for getting your ideas accepted. (All too often, even great ideas need to be sold.)

Ethos

A distinguished character, moral nature, or a guiding belief in a purpose. What does ethos do when you use it? It establishes credibility. For example, Nordstroms department stores' reputation and demonstrated values of service and quality over many years give them high creditability.

Pathos

An element in experience or artistic representation evoking compassion and identification. In use it means getting someone emotionally involved. The memorable Disney character Bambi involves pathos through emotion that people never forget.

Logos

Pointing distinctly to the origin and logical progression of something. The use is establishing the logic behind something.

GREEK IDEATION TECHNIQUES

Ethos	Guiding principles, basic beliefs, character	Establish Credibility
Pathos	Elements involving relating to someone; sympathy	The Emotions Involved
Logos	The Progression of something	The Logic Behind It
Lexis	Words to be used, Diction	Chosen and Selected
Taxis	Sentence structure, and presentation form	Order of Ethos, Pathos, Logos

For example, the FAA imposes exact, precise standards for pilots in order to insure safety.

Lexis

Deciding what language and what words to use as it pertains to ethos, pathos, and logos. The selection of language is critical for achieving effective communication.

Taxis

Deciding on the sentence structure and combinations of sentence composition to be used with in conjunction with ethos, pathos, and logos.

Ethos, pathos and logos come to us from the ancient Greeks. These elements are described as Greek Ideation Techniques, the creative thinking techniques used to broaden our thinking, especially with attention to language and presentation. They are also used in marketing products and establishing brand identification by advertisers.

Our interpretation of their meaning takes liberties in usage with respect to their philosophical meanings. Ethos is established through the reputation of what you do and becomes the foundation of your credibility. Pathos is becoming emotionally involved or sympathetic in what we are doing. Logos is the logic behind it and why it works. Associated with ethos, pathos and logos is lexis, that is, the language you have chosen to use in describing the ethos, pathos and logos. And finally, taxis is the order in which you present ethos, pathos, logos, and lexis.

When and how do we determine the appropriate use of these concepts? If you're working with a group of bankers or accountants, presenting the logic first is often more effective. Logos will also help your ethos (credibility). Employing ethos, pathos and logos helps you to stay out of the box and raise the bar.

We see examples of Greek Philosophy applied in today's world. Our friend, Val Halamanderis, President of The National Association for HomeCare, places great emphasis on establishing ethos, pathos and logos in their work of caring for people. Here are a few ways he and the National Association for HomeCare's staff achieve higher standards in their work.

1. Reinvent yourself; alter your DNA. You may not realize it, but you have the opportunity to change your habits and maybe even the ability to alter your genetic makeup. Most of us understand that scientists in a laboratory can do this. Less well known, however, is the fact that genetic adaptations also occur spontaneously. When a chimpanzee steps beyond his DNA and learns to use a tool which no member of his species has done before, the revolutionary behavior gets passed down in his genes to his offspring who exemplify the "learned" physical and behavioral characteristics. What this extreme example demonstrates is that you can be whatever or whoever you want to be within the realm of truth. Nikos Kazantzakis wrote, "If you don't like your life, change it." You are the artist. You have the paints and the brushes. You are defined by your habits. Decide who you want to be from your teeth to your toes. Pick six people from whom you would like to borrow elements, and integrate these qualities into your life. Keeping their photos in front of you will facilitate this transfer.

Double your brain power and harness your subconscious. Albert Einstein wrote that human beings use less than 10 percent of their brain. The potential of the human mind is infinite, and yet most people barely use theirs before dying. Dr. Joseph Salvatore, a forward-thinking professor, taught us how to make greater use of the subconscious mind. The way it works is simple. The conscious mind will direct the subconscious to work out a particular nettlesome problem and demand the answer to the riddle be given at a certain time, usually at 7:30 a.m. in the morning. Almost without fail, the subconscious will come through like a radio alarm clock with the answer to the tough question at the appointed hour. Because of this experience, we know that others can program and use their subconscious minds in the same way.

2. Look for CQ along with IQ. In the hiring practices, many corporations look for employees with experience and a high IQ. There is nothing wrong with this; native intelligence is very much a desirable trait. However, even more important than this is an individual's caring quotient. Inasmuch as caring is the great secret of the universe, you cannot have too many caring employees. Look for signs that the potential employee is unselfish. What do they do in their free time? To what extent do they understand the importance of giving back to the community and serving others? If selfishness and greed spell destruction for any organization, the unselfishness and caring produce prosperity and unimagined success.

3. Never hire anyone who isn't smarter than you. The essence of any organization or institution depends on teamwork. Anyone who is hired must make a substantial contribution to the whole. Some leaders and managers are insecure and will not bring into the organization anyone that they cannot dominate. This is a mistake because it ensures the level of performance of the organization will always be modest. Individuals who are hired should bring a dimension that compliments the efforts of others. A company that hires the best and the brightest people is enriched by them. At the same time it is essential that each employee have the same high values and goals, and is committed to the greater good.

4. Always hire up. Whenever an employee has left our company, either for the improvement of their personal circumstances or due to some unresolvable conflict in values, we have made it a habit to use the opportunity to hire someone who is even better and more talented. In this way, the organization will become stronger with each loss.

5. Get the team the tools they need to do the job. A major part of the executive's job is to identify the tools that the team needs to do the job better, and to help secure these. This involves research, staying on the cutting edge of new technology, and good judgment. New purchases must be useful not only in the present but also for many years to come. Unfortunately, employees do not always know what they need. An interoffice team will usually help sort this out.

You *can* make a silk purse out of a sow's ear!

"You can't make a silk purse out of a sow's ear" has been a friendly admonition for years. Yet people make silk purses out of sows' ears every day. Organizations are faced with a bad situation or a poor product, and they turn them around to become successful again.

Making a silk purse from a sow's ear requires creative input and thinking. It requires vision. You must be able to dissect problems realistically, to see the opportunity that a positive change could create. You have to check the validity of your vision or solutions because you can fail if you kid yourselves by denying reality.

Our long time friend, George Fink, who is president of a major company, had a company that was really like a sow's ear from the start. However, he wanted to correct the flaws and make it into a silk purse. Through applying the strategies we're talking about, he raised the standards of performance of the company. They performed at a high level, which set new standards for the entire industry. Later, he sold it to one of the biggest companies in its field for a big payoff. Most noteworthy of all, the employees participated in the payday!

George Fink's skilled leadership demonstrated that you can raise the bar and you can make a silk purse out of a sow's ear. He learned first hand that you must see the qualities in the sow's ear that could be molded into a silk purse. If positive attributes are buried in the negative, without cultivation, reorganization would be very difficult. Turning performance around becomes nearly impossible.

Getting unclogged

It's important to have a lust for life: to see a beautiful sunset, to climb a mountain, or ski down a challenging slope. There are too many of us who sit in a corner while our arteries are getting clogged up. The results are we end up with clogged up people. Clogging affects us both physically and mentally. Companies who have recreation time and think time built into their daily routine do better. They keep their minds and bodies in top shape. And yet, even to this day, when we are placing emphasis on health, it's a practice that few organizations even talk about or acknowledge. We get unclogged by getting into the action, getting involved, and by using our skills.

Disney Studios, for example, has one of the most complete exercise facilities in corporate America...and it's been in existence since the 1930s! Every kind of exercise equipment you can imagine is available. Not only do they make it available to their employees, they encourage them to use it. This recreational facility assures a balance between the mental and physical. Mike describes a typical scene at Disney Studio: "At lunch time, you can walk down Mickey Mouse Drive and Dopey Avenue, where you'll see people playing Ping-Pong, volleyball, softball, and sitting on park benches. There is a gym with a running track, steam room, card room, snack bar, and exercise equipment."

Put it on the line

We call the symbol on the next page an "AOL" button. No, it doesn't have anything to do with America Online. The fact that

the line is a line is clear to everyone who sees it for the first time. However, a few people mistake what sits on the line with an upside down McDonald's arch. That it is not. But when an audience sees the symbol on a flip chart, someone inevitably shouts out the slang word for derriere. People often jump up from their seats shouting "That's what we need around here, people who will put it on the line." What kind of special people are these individuals? Where do they come from? What motivates them to put it on the line?

The leadership teaching of Taoism says that we should develop the personal qualities of vitality, energy, and spirit to have a full life. And it requires that we have all three of these attributes to put it on the line. Further, we added three additional characteristics—dedication, risk-taking, and resolution. These personal qualities are why emphasis is placed today on the importance of values and beliefs as they reflect the passion of a person who will stick their neck out.

Experience indicates that those who believe in their cause enough to take a stance are people who are truly involved. They actively participate in the give and take process, rather than being viewed as a mere onlooker. Consequently, communication flows freely up and down and across boundaries in relationships. Motivation and esprit de corps is high because of people's deeply held beliefs. The result is people become inspired and will out-think and out-work the competition.

If we want people to willingly put it on the line, we must involve them in a cause that they deeply believe in. We must inform them about what is going on and inspire them with meritorious examples.

There are countless examples of individuals, companies, and nations that have put it on the line. We have one in our friend Gary Wendt, former chairman of GE Capital. Gary built one of the strongest, most profitable companies in one of the shortest periods of time by raising the bar. His leadership skills have caused people to want to put it on the line. He sets an example by sticking his neck out frequently, by taking risks, by trying, by starting initiatives that put it on the line everyday, by doing things that raise the bar. Call us if you would like to know about our many motivational buttons!

Principles for raising the bar: Strategy #5

✓ Solve this year's problems by creating new solutions—not last year's solutions.
✓ Figure out how to get into the Creative Zone.
✓ Utilize ideation techniques to produce breakthroughs.
✓ Get unclogged.
✓ Put it on the line in order to achieve breakthroughs.
✓ Know how to see your idea.

Personal applications

How to get warm

A number of years ago we were doing a considerable amount of work in Los Angeles with a number of our clients and got a corporate apartment there.

Diane had flown in to Los Angeles to facilitate a one-week project planning charrette for a client. Needless to say, Diane planned to spend very little time at the apartment (sleep, shower, and shove off). She noticed the day of her arrival, however, that the apartment was ice-cold.

Therefore, she cranked up the heating thermostat. When she woke the next morning, it was like a freezer in the apartment. It was so cold, that when she talked, white mist poured out of her mouth. She called the maintenance department of the apartment complex and left a message on the answering machine to check out the heating system because she was freezing.

After completing another day's work, she arrived back at the apartment and noticed immediately that the air was colder yet! She decided to high tail it down to the maintenance department to find out what they had discovered.

The problem was a broken part in the heating system, one that was out of stock. The repair people told Diane that they would have to special order the replacement part. Diane then asked a fundamental question—*when* could they replace the part. They said they would order the part and could expect to have it in for her the next day. Diane thought that there would only be one more day of ice cold air to live with in the apartment.

The next day came and the heater was still not fixed. Diane proceeded to march down to the maintenance office to see *why* they had not fixed the heater. They said the part didn't arrive. Diane asked if they could actually go *get* the part, as it was bitterly cold. (She knew this was asking much of a company who claimed to be service oriented). They reassured her that they would try to go get the needed part.

Diane was not feeling convinced by the responses that they would try hard to go get the part. But she thought, "Have faith."

She returned that night to discover the problem still existed after three freezing days. Although they didn't know it, people in the maintenance office were about to experience an Italian temper (namely, Diane's). However, during her march down to the maintenance office she stopped. She knew she would have to think out of the box and try to solve the problem herself. Solving this problem the conventional way, ordering a new part, did not work. Trying to solve problems using old conventional ways often had not worked. This caused Diane to stop her march in order to *think.* She thought, "what I need here is a breakthrough solution, otherwise I'll freeze again tonight. The goal is not to freeze again!" Her mission was to find the part. Who would have the part? Then the solution hit her.

"Eureka! Another apartment would have the part," she thought. So, she skipped the march and ran down to the maintenance department with excitement. She patiently listened to the maintenance people tell her their story about why they couldn't go get the part. There were lots of wonderful excuses. After Diane had heard enough she said, "Could I please go see the model apartment that you show perspective tenants?" They said, "Sure, follow us," not having a clue as to what she was up to. They all arrived at the model apartment, which felt blessedly warm as they entered. Diane went over to the closet housing the heater and opened it. She said, "Show me the part here that is the same one that is broken in ours." They proceeded to point out the part to Diane. Then she said, "Now take the part out and put it in ours until the one you ordered arrives."

Their first reaction was an expression that translated as "What? That would mean work!" Then they looked at Diane and knew that the look on her face meant "do it or die!" Her facilitation skills came in handy, she made sure they took the right part out, walked them over to the apartment, watched them install it, and stayed until she made sure heat was coming out of the furnace unit.

Sometimes, breakthrough solutions have immediate—and soulwarming—benefits.

❑ STRATEGY #6:
Communicate and Organize

"Have something really worthwhile to say and people will listen."
–Dr. Norman Vincent Peale

Advice from a pro

There is no doubt that the late Dr. Norman Vincent Peale, minister and author of the bestseller *The Power of Positive Thinking*, was one of the finest communicators of this century. He was a member of an elite club that includes the likes of Sir Winston Churchill and President Franklin D. Roosevelt. These men were the best. Few others would be rated as good. Most of us would just get by in this demanding field.

An avid reader on the topic of speaking and training, Mike credits Dr. Peale with the best advice he ever received about public speaking. Mike says:

"Dr. Peale was truly a great speaker. He created excitement by arousing your passions; he challenged you and made you a true believer. He was fun. He had an inimitable style that made his stories come to life. I heard him speak as a freshman. I joined the same chapter of Phi Gamma Delta at Ohio Wesleyan that he was a member of; I attended his Marble Collegiate Church in New York City; and I spoke on the same platform with him on many occasions. Dr. Peale gave me some wonderful advice about how to speak.

He said, "First, always have something to say about something you have experienced personally. Avoid using too many quotes from other people. Speak from your own background. Don't worry or fuss about the way you look or stand, or gesture, or sound. Get up and talk as you would naturally.

"If you have something to say, keep saying it over and over, and a unique style will emerge. Too many speakers worry about the superficial aspects of communicating, trying to force a certain style. People respond to those who are real and sincere rather than studied and fake. Listen to the quality of your message; deliver your ideas while standing in front of a mirror.

"Speak every chance you get, to practically any type of group. You can't become a professional at anything by doing it once a week. Do it over and over until it is second nature, like breathing out and breathing in. Collect anything and everything related to your work as a speaker; soon you will have a large collection of gifts that will reinforce your commitment and remind you of how far you've come."

Dr. Peale reveled in recalling the gifts that he has received over the years. He left us with a gift that we call "Peale's Rules":

1. Focus on what you say more than how you say it.
2. Try not to use notes, and whatever you do, never read from them on a teleprompter.
3. Look at your audience and respond to their feelings; make eye contact.
4. Have your audience well-lighted and stand in a well-lighted spot yourself, so that your audience is not in the dark.
5. Don't tell tired jokes. Don't tell any jokes if you're not good at it. Stick with situational humor and with laughing at yourself.
6. Get your facts right!

The 6 white doves

There is a story told by Kahlil Gibran (and other traditional storytellers) about six white doves that visited a village that had prospered for many, many years. The village people were skilled craftsmen and artisans who looked forward to the return of these beautiful doves each year, just as the residents of San Juan Capistrano await the return of the swallows. The village people would tell this story:

"Every year in our valley six identical, perfectly matched white doves come that fly in a "V" formation. On the wing tip of just one of the white doves, there is a tiny black dot."

Everybody in the village notices that black dot on the one wing tip of the one white dove because of its bold contrast with the rest of the snowy white feathers. One year, as people communicate and tell the story, a change begins to occur and eventually the story sounds like this:

"Every spring to our valley come six of the most beautiful black doves that you have ever seen. These doves are charcoal black except on the wing tip of just one of the doves is a small white dot."

What happened? Everyone agrees that there were doves, that there were six of them, and that only one had a spot, yet the details changed. The six white doves, through the passing of time and the distortion of communications, were described as black doves, with one having a white spot instead of a black spot.

Repetition and the passing of time can often cause a complete misrepresentation of facts. This can be very dangerous! Suppose someone's life were hanging in the balance? Suppose the outcome of a murder trial depended on the accurate recollection of the color of the doves?

Dr. Peale was right—You have to get your facts right!

Speaking and informing

Most of us use the art of speaking every day in our business dealings, whether we're interacting one on one, addressing a small group, or talking to a large group. Still, little formal training is given for what we call transitional speaking—communicating in daily transactions with people. That's truly a shame.

Creative ideas often wither and die on the vine because of poor communication. These ideas are like a big trophy fish that is hooked...but not reeled into the boat.

Or look at it from another way: We can't successfully bake a cake without the crucial information we need to bake the cake—the recipe. Without the right communication, we end up with either a bowl of raw cake mix...or sometimes, with a burnt cake.

Ideas need clear, understandable communication if the plan is to be carried out successfully. Nothing hurts a team's performance more than developing a group strategy, detailing the plays, and then mixing up the signals as you're preparing to execute the plan with them. Is there anything more deflating than a great plan that's delivered by someone who speaks poorly?

We're talking about people who seem to have stones in their mouths, who somehow make good messages lose all meaning. After such people address groups, you frequently hear audience members say things like, "What the heck just happened?" What happened was the appointed spokesperson didn't communicate correctly.

Visual aids and notes

One good way to improve communications is to use visual aids. Speakers, leaders, and teachers have used slides, tapes, overheads, and notes effectively for many years. Computerized slide-shows have now been added to the electronic arsenal of communicating. Each of these techniques can be used to enhance getting the message across, but each must be selected with care.

It's important to bear in mind that spontaneous creativity is what makes speakers exciting, dynamic, and natural. Spontaneous creativity wins over an audience and makes our efforts worthwhile. Of course, there are specific occasions (such as legal depositions), where we want materials to be exact. However, as a general rule, spontaneity is far more powerful.

Dr. Peale suggests that speakers can become too dependent on written notes and mechanical aids. Overreliance on these tools slows your pace and often results in a presentation that is too deliberate to be effective. When you rely heavily on notes and aids, they reduce your ability to let spontaneous creativity occur.

Therefore, we suggest using aids and visuals to support what you are saying, rather than to drive what you are saying. If you find that you must click ahead to the next slide in order to know what to say next—your presentation is being driven by the aids and not by you.

Mike's artifacts and flip charts

So what can you do if you don't memorize your notes or have overheads and other support materials? Mike has developed a technique that allows spontaneous communication, while at the same time provides some visual support. He often places two tables on a stage or in a room where he is to speak or teach. On those tables he places all types of artifacts. Each artifact is an item that reminds him of a concept he plans to talk about. Each object acts like a console on a pipe organ, with each one serving as a stop on the organ. He picks up different artifacts as he's speaking, and these are eventually incorporated into his talk. This approach allows for a lot of spontaneity, as the artifacts act as guideposts.

Mike recently gave an interview in which he spoke at some length about this technique. Here's what he had to say:

"Artifact speaking makes a concept more vivid for people. If I'm discussing the concept of working with color, called color lining, I have a four-colored pen on my artifact table. If I'm talking about Displayed Thinking and how it works, I've got examples and pictures of people using the Displayed Thinking system. And when Diane and I are teaching together, she will put up overhead transparencies or multimedia presentations using PowerPoint that support what I'm saying. For instance, if I am talking about a Team Center, I've got layouts of various Team Centers we've designed for organizations. Artifact speaking enables me to talk fast, not forgetting content, but with spontaneity that keeps the creative doors open. It works because I'm not programmed into a predetermined pattern or approach.

"The broad categories that we speak about today started like a little acorn that continues to grow, just like our interests and experiences. The tree continues to keep filling up with more and more acorns as we grow. I read continually, and as a result, I have stored up both general and specific knowledge to draw upon in my presentations. Yet many ideas just pop out as I am talking, using artifact speaking to stay open to new concepts. You don't really know exactly where new ideas come from. They're a little like Mozart's music; he simply heard notes in his mind and wrote them down.

"Another old standby tool that I use to support my speaking is flip charts. I take a lot of kidding from Diane about the flip charts—she says they really show my age. But the truth is that they never break down, nor do they need any electricity, and I'm always free to compose quickly, with no boot-up time (except for my brain!). The flip charts that I use are not necessarily for the audience to see and I even tell people this. The charts are there for me to sketch and write ideas on as I go along.

"I call this 'flip chart tracking.' The charts help me to arrange my thoughts, as well as keep account of what I've said. These two concepts, artifact speaking and flip chart tracking, help me to stimulate my imagination and document what I have done. There's an added benefit: audience members will come up during the breaks to see the artifacts which, in effect, become exhibits that promote interaction and participation in a natural way."

Good communication in action

The Stone Center of New Jersey is a state-of-the-art kidney stone treatment facility. The Center has been affiliated with the Creative Thinking Association for many years, and its people have utilized our communication tools and techniques to raise the bar both in their organization and in the profession of medicine.

Arlyn Rayfield and her team at the Stone Center developed a new working (and living) philosophy after one of our "Think Out of the Box" seminars: "Whatever it Takes." They call this philosophy WIT for short; they keep their WITs about them at all times, and they only hire people who appear to have the WIT mentality.

They treat patients as though they were guests in their own home. The waiting room at the Stone Center is called the Family Room; patient representatives are trained to treat patients courteously at all times, and to visit and spend time in the Family Room. (A truly human connection is an important part of one-on-one communication, after all.)

Mediocrity is not acceptable at the Stone Center. Arlyn's people stress this concept repeatedly during the employee orientation process, and throughout day-to-day activities at the Center. The standards are set at one hundred percent, period. Here's an example of how well that message was communicated:

Recently, The Joint Commission on the Accreditation of Healthcare Organizations (JCAH) came to inspect the Stone Center facilities. After six months of intense preparations, and two days of grueling inspections, the Center received a score of 99 out of 100. The staff exercised their right to contest the inspector's findings, because they genuinely believed that they deserved a score of 100, and as a result, 99 percent simply was not acceptable to them.

After contesting the score, the staff members succeeded in winning a score of 100—with commendation. (That, by the way, is the highest rating the JCAH can give.)

Arlyn's team treats all patients as if they will be coming back to visit again in the future. They strive to be better than the best, not simply "one of the best." Team members are challenged to "think continuously" and to avoid individual and collective stagnation. They're constantly raising the bar!

Every year, they create a Master Plan. They evaluate what needs to be done, what has not been completed from the previous year, and what has been completed. From this, they develop a new master plan for the upcoming year. The entire management team is involved in this process, and the staff is kept "in the loop" as to what the master plan is. The plan is also reviewed throughout the year, and updated as needed.

At Stone Center, every management and staff meeting begins with creativity exercise—a training puzzle that relates to situations occurring at the Center. Just as intriguing, the Center has incorporated HUGGs into their daily routine. These are components of the daily briefing. HUGG stands for:

> Huddle.
> Update.
> Go on your way.
> Get it done!

Management at Stone Center ends all meetings with an Open Forum session. All employees are encouraged (and coached, if necessary) to communicate about issues of concern during this time period. This practice encourages the feeling of being "part of the team," and it's also excellent experience for practicing public speaking.

Constant improvement in communication is an important goal at Stone Center. Through the use of Master Plans, Briefing Boards, and Daily Briefings that feature plenty of HUGGs, Stone Center has established itself as a superior healthcare facility with a well-deserved reputation for putting the patient first.

Speaking as a team leader

Speaking as a team leader is not the same as before an audience filled with people who may or may not know you. Your team members have probably "got your number." Credibility may be an overworked word, but without it, team leadership is nearly impossible.

Therefore, the issue of character is germane in a discussion of effective leadership through speaking and communicating. Our national values have been confused of late; some have argued that one's personal life does not effect one's ability to lead others. This point of view undermines leadership, because being credible is a requirement for getting people to follow. This is not to say that leaders must be puritan in their behavior. However, our national politics have demonstrated that there is a line of common decency that can't be crossed over if we're going to be truly effective in influencing others. There must be some conformity to standards of taste, propriety, and etiquette.

You will hear it said today that everybody lies about everything. This is a tragic commentary on the state of our values! How sad is it that the justification is essentially true! Let's resolve to stop lying. We should be willing to become Boy Scouts and Girl Scouts again; we should start by telling the truth.

The underlying principle for speaking as a team leader is to have the character that will cause people to believe in you and trust your judgment. In accordance with this fundamental principle, we suggest these rules:

Rules for calling team plays

1. Concept and example

Clearly state the concept behind any action or idea that you wish to initiate. Clarify the meaning of the concept by giving an example of it that illuminates our understanding. Concepts that aren't clarified by example remain vague and uninteresting.

Example: Windows never get dirty in our restaurants (picture of clean window). Picture showing windows being washed before they are even dirty.

2. Instructions (signals) are clear

Instructions are followed when they are simple and symbolic, not wordy. **Example:** If we want someone to turn left at the next crossroads, we show that instruction as a symbol, rather than as a long paragraph written in tiny type.

3. Team ready to play

Develop methods to test out if the team is ready and prepared to play. Conduct a test run that can be evaluated. **Example:** A scuba diving team can be tested in a tank before actually entering the ocean.

4. Play sent mnemonically

Select letters to make up the parts of a definition that form a word. **Example:** The most famous is KISS, keep it simple, stupid.

5. Send in plays

The team leader should have plays or strategies in mind to offer the team.

6. Correct the plan during play

The strong team leader will correct faulty plays very quickly.

7. Anticipate the next play

Anticipating the next play is the responsibility of every team leader. This is also known as "anticipatory design strategy" (ADS).

Organizing for communications flow

We want to form guidelines that will assure a union between team members and customers. These are organizing principles to help facilitate information flow. They offer us ways to marshal the troops and get them ready for action.

Nobody has a corner on brains

Within a team, everyone will have something to contribute if there's a chance to do so. Often, the problem is simply that the organization doesn't have a method that allows for people to participate. They have no method that allows people to give input, suggestions, and ideas.

You never know where a good idea is going to come from. We recommend the Displayed Thinking system as a way to allow others to see, at a glance, where you are and how they can participate in what you're doing.

How to communicate and organize projects

So often, we find organizations developing great master plans, and detailing all the ideas, but not executing them correctly. This is often due to poor communication of the organizational details of the project. Understand that the "C" and "O" elements of the

MICORBS functions must be planned and executed. Here are examples of the communications and organizational Displayed Thinking boards:

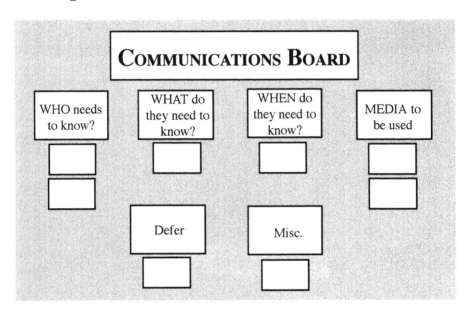

The Communications function of the MICORBS model must ask and answer the following basic questions:

> ➤ Who needs to know?
> ➤ What do they need to know?
> ➤ When do they need to know it?
> ➤ What media will be used to communicate that?

The Organizational function of the MICORBS model must ask and answer the following questions:

> ➤ What needs to be done?
> ➤ When does it need to be done?
> ➤ Who is going to do it?
> ➤ What resources (if any) do they need to accomplish the task?

Apotheosis—the Ideal

The Apotheosis, or the Ideal, was designed and developed as a leadership program that would illuminate exactly what leaders need to be aware of when working with people. This concept is also applicable to all of us in our daily lives. The Apotheosis concept embodies four major areas around which communications ideas cluster.

1. **Hurt:** When dealing with other people it is important to remember that we all hurt from something simply because we are all humans. So, as a leader or a lover, when you know someone is hurting, you must do your best to help them heal. To help people to heal simply by your sensitivity and recognition of their hurting is called empathy. So when you discover someone who is hurt, try to help him or her to heal.

2. **Fulfillment:** We all have a longing for fulfillment. We want to make our mark. We are dreamers. Everyone that you deal with has this longing. When someone has this longing for fulfillment, assist him or her to satisfy their longing.

3. **Help:** We all need help along the way. The reason we all need help is that nobody is smart enough today to do anything alone. We all need help because all humans are imperfect. When somebody needs help, teach him or her. Teach somebody how to improve his or her skills. Help them to lift the bar personally with the skills that you can expose them to.

4. **Opportunity:** We all need a break. It isn't easy to get things started, to get careers going. We're all interdependent today. So if you're in a leadership position, give someone an opportunity to succeed. Or be a "friend at court" where you speak out for or on behalf of another person.

THE APOTHEOSIS

By Mike Vance & Diane Deacon

We all **HURT** from something, we're human.

We all **LONG** for fulfillment, we're dreamers.

We all need **HELP** along the way, we're imperfect.

We all need a **BREAK** on the journey, we're interdependent.

–As a leader or lover–

HEAL someone by your sensitivity,

ASSIST someone to satisfy their longing,

TEACH someone how to improve their skills,

GIVE someone an opportunity to succeed.

The desire

Create the desire in others who want what it is that you have. But don't just give it to them; teach them how to get it. That's what Tom Sawyer did. A classic example is when Aunt Molly told Tom to whitewash the fence. Well, Tom was an organizer and he wanted to get all his buddies in the neighborhood to whitewash the fence so he could sit back, eat an apple, and go fishing—and Tom knew how to motivate people. He had a sore toe with a big huge bandage on it. He told one of the younger boys, who looked up to him, that if he helped Tom to whitewash the fence, he would let him see that hurt big toe. Since the younger fellow was in such awe of Tom, and since he wanted to see that big toe, he took Tom's instruction on whitewashing the fence! Tom acted effectively on the young fellow's desire.

Principles for raising the bar: Strategy #6

✓ Have something to say.
✓ Get the right information out to the right people at the right time.
✓ Use open methods to allow others to give input, suggestions, and ideas.
✓ Plan how you will communicate and organize projects and ideas.
✓ Be sensitive when communicating with others.

Personal applications

Some of the best

We have selected what we consider some of the very finest examples of speaking, informing, and organizing for your personal application of the concepts, discussed as part of Strategy #6. We suggest that you read each one in a quiet place and allow enough time to contemplate their deep meaning following your reading. It is also helpful to read these passages aloud to someone else and discuss their importance as documents of history.

Speaking (communicating)

Abraham Lincoln's Gettysburg Address:

"Four score and seven years ago, our fathers brought forth upon this continent a new nation, conceived in liberty and dedicated to the proposition that all men are created equal.

"Now we are engaged in a great civil war, testing whether that nation or any nation so conceived and so dedicated can long endure. We are met on a great battlefield of that war. We are met to dedicate a portion of it as the final resting place of those who here gave their lives that our nation might live. It is altogether fitting and proper that we should do this. But in a larger sense, we cannot dedicate, we cannot consecrate, we cannot hallow this ground.

"The brave men living and dead who struggled here have consecrated it far above our poor power to add or detract. The world will little note nor long remember what we say here, but it can never forget what they did here. It is for us, the living, rather to be dedicated here to the unfinished work that they have thus far so nobly advanced. It is rather for us to be here dedicated to the great task remaining before us—that from these honored dead we take increased devotion to that cause for which they have given the last full measure of devotion—that we here highly resolve that the dead will not have died in vain—that the nation, under God, have a new birth of freedom—and that government of the people, by the people, and for the people, shall not perish from the earth."

Informing

President Franklin D. Roosevelt's message, calling for war against Japan, December 8, 1941 (Abridged):

"Yesterday, December 7, 1941—a date which will live in infamy—the United States of America was suddenly and deliberately attacked by naval and air force of the Empire of Japan.

"As Commander-in-Chief of the army and navy, I have directed that all measures be taken for our defense. No matter how long it may take us to overcome this premeditated invasion, the American people in their righteous might will win through to absolute victory.

"I believe I interpret the will of the Congress and of the people when I assert that we will not only defend ourselves to the utter most, but will make very certain that this form of treachery shall never endanger us again.

"Hostilities exist. There is no blinking at the fact that our people, our territory, and our interests are in grave danger.

"With confidence in our armed forces—with the unbounded determination of our people—will gain the inevitable triumph—so help us God.

"I ask that the Congress declare that since the unprovoked and dastardly attack by Japan on Sunday, December seventh, a state of war has existed between the United States and the Japanese Empire."

Organizing

Preamble of The Constitution of the United States:

"We the people of the United States, in order to form a more perfect union, establish justice, insure domestic tranquillity, provide for the common defense, promote the general welfare, and secure the blessings of liberty to ourselves and our posterity, do ordain and establish this Constitution of the United States of America."

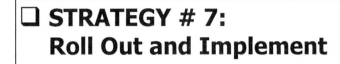

❏ STRATEGY # 7:
Roll Out and Implement

"Always be on time and under budget."
–Mike and Diane

Winning the war

"Our major competitor is ferocious! We must launch a major attack, a plan so superior that it will blow them away, far away from us! This is war!"

Such were the words that launched the campaign of a major American consumer products corporation not long ago. The company had been fighting strategic battles with its major competitor for years, but this time the fight had become downright ugly. "Pull out all the stops!" was the order of the day.

There was an unspoken motto, too: "All's fair in love and war." A division of this company asked us to work on a plan to win the so-called war. These folks did not want just any plan—they wanted a plan that would deliver the ultimate blow, a plan of superior thinking that would put them so far ahead that it would take the competition a long, long time to catch up. The team leader had the spirit, the passion, the leadership qualities, and the credibility to inspire his team to rise to the occasion.

We scheduled a three-day charrette, during which we facilitated the master plan for the project. From there, we continued to develop the details of the MICORBS process to make sure we had a rock-solid plan of attack. This required six days of work packed into three longs days. We kept pizza and drinks coming nonstop until we had unanimously agreed on the final version of the plan.

It was an unforgettable experience! However, a plan is just a plan. It sits on a shelf unless a rollout program is implemented to launch the ideas. The next step, then, was to deliver a comprehensive launch plan. Step by step, day by day, month by month, we spelled out exactly how we would deliver what was, after all, a superior program. We ended up with more than 100 Displayed Thinking Boards that told the story. Everyone agreed upon the plan of attack, including their individual roles and specific responsibilities. When members of upper management were briefed, they agreed with what we had put together. "Ramp up and go with it," they instructed.

That's what happened. The plan was executed with exceptional speed and rolled out as we had projected—nearly picture-perfect! Why? Because when you execute a well-prepared plan as a team, you're extremely hard to beat! (This company's major competitor would attest to that.)

That rollout raised the bar in that industry to a level that had yet to be achieved by competitors in the industry. A new era had begun.

Successful rollouts

Many projects fail to get off the ground because no one develops a plan on how to implement the project. The number of projects that fall into this category is huge.

Successful rollouts, on the other hand, usually share certain characteristics. First, they have a master plan that includes a *launch plan.* The launch plan specifies how people will roll out the project. Second, everyone agrees to and pledges their commitment to the plan. Third, people think through and plan for contingencies by spelling out the "what ifs." Fourth, team members check the plan continually to see if it meets the goals and objectives of the master plan. Fifth, management establishes rewards and incentives for bringing the plan in ahead of schedule and under budget. And sixth, there's a theme and appropriate symbolism to foster spirit and communicate the ideas behind the strategy.

Roll Out and Implement

Let's assume that you've used your new skills and techniques to think out of the box and develop innovative ideas and plans for a project. Now it's time to make the plans a reality. It's time to implement them. It's time to roll them out.

Possibly the greatest example of a rollout plan was the massive invasion of Europe. VE Day has become the supreme example of an ideal rollout when the allies from many diverse countries collaborated to think out of the box for this invasion. The purpose was to preserve the world's freedom by assembling the biggest army in the history of mankind, and was trained to roll out in one gigantic joint effort to invade Normandy and stop the German war machine. The result was the creation of perhaps the grandest master plan that has ever been executed. This invasion became a model for complicated and successful rollouts.

The following conditions must be met to consider a rollout truly successful: The communications and organizational plan must be completed as discussed in Strategy #6. Next, you must identify the "to do's," tasks that need to be done and who needs to do them. The Displayed Thinking system must be used to help visualize and walk through a detailed plan step by step.

The communications and organization components of the MICORBS phases, with the tasks and assignments, should be placed on a time line board. Start out with the exact month you will begin putting the tasks into action. Then go across the board and put up all of the months until you reach the target rollout month. Then place each of the task cards directly under the month in which they are to be completed. You can also specify under each month the amount of resources that will be needed. These details will contribute to the success of the project.

After you have completed the rollout plan, step back and look at it again from beginning to end. It should tell a story of the tasks to be done, who will do them, and when and what will be needed to accomplish the task. Don't forget to get commitment from everyone whose name is on the board!

An effective plan will tell a clear story and offer a satisfactory answer to the question, "Is this rollout doable?"

Displayed Thinking®

DATE ___ MO ___ / ___ DAY ___ / ___ YR ___
PAGE ___ OF ___
TIME ___ a.m. ___ p.m.

APPLICATIONS

☐ Note Taking ☐ Project Master Plans
☐ Daily Itineraries ☐ Idea Development
☐ Phone Messages ☐ Communications
☐ Financial Plan/Budget ☐ Organization
☐ Meeting/Participants ☐ Miscellaneous

TOPIC

Time Frame/Implementation Schedule

SUBJECT	SUBJECT	SUBJECT	SUBJECT	SUBJECT	SUBJECT	SUBJECT
Communications	Organization	Miscellaneous	Month	Month	Month	Month
DETAILS	DETAILS	DETAILS	DETAILS	DETAILS	DETAILS	DETAILS
WHO needs to know?	WHAT needs to be done?	Briefings				
WHAT do they need to know?	WHEN does it need to be done?	Target Dates				
WHEN do they need to know?	WHO is going to do it?	Major Events				
MEDIA to be used?	Miscellaneous					
Miscellaneous						

Action Codes: Do ☒, Doing ☒, Done ☒, Urgent ■, Call ☒, Question ☒, Miscellaneous ☐ _____

© MCMLXXXV Intellectual Equities, Inc. 16600 Sprague Road, Suite 120
Cleveland, Ohio 44130 (440) 243-8015 1-800-445-6477

R-24

What it looks like in action

We were working with a large retail chain to develop its annual merchandise and marketing plan. The challenging goals of the plan were to increase sales, cut costs, and differentiate the chain from the competition by raising the bar of standards in the industry. We had completed the development of the plan using the MICORBS process. The master plan, idea development, communications and organizational plans, retrieval, briefing, and synapse boards were all done. Having selected the right team and having the correct planning tools enabled us to complete this complex process in a three-day, facilitated charrette. The plan itself looked promising and everyone was excited about it.

From the plan, we laid out a 52-week merchandising and marketing time line board. Across the top of the board, each week of the year was listed. Under the week we placed colored-coded cards identifying the merchandise to be launched and the marketing that would promote the merchandise. In addition, under each month were green cards identifying the amount of money that would be spent, along with projections of income and profits.

That board told a complete story! Sometimes, you'll find that the Displayed Thinking process will uncover unexpected weak links in planning or communication, as this one clearly did. The original plan called for a $30 million advertising budget during these 52 weeks. Members from the advertising agency were present during the planning session, but they kept their arms folded most of the time, giving the distinct impression that they really didn't want to be involved. We asked them to add their advertising budget to the time line rollout board on green cards.

This told us a surprising story. All $30 million was slated to be spent in the first three months of the year! This was either a very strange new advertising "concept," or a sign that the advertising team really wasn't engaged in the planning process. When we finished the plan and briefed the chairman of the company, he told the advertising people in no uncertain terms that they would not be permitted to spend the *total* advertising budget in the first quarter. With this the advertising team unfolded their arms, muttered some interesting language, and really started to partici-pate in the process for the first time.

"See what you are doing!"

Walt Disney said, "If more people could see what they are doing, they might think twice about doing it." He was right!

The process we're talking about enables you to see the plan and make many needed changes. For example, we have suc-cessfully facilitated this process with numerous pharmaceutical companies when they launch new products. As you probably know, new drug approval can be a very slow and lengthy process. Therefore, when the company projects the dates and schedules in the FDA's approval process, we go to work on the rollout launch plan. Figure out how you can expedite the process. In this case, and with many other projects, the details from every division must be planned and coordinated together.

For example, the various plans from the manufacturing, packaging, training, marketing, and advertising teams must be detailed, communicated, and agreed upon before executing. When we can see the plan, then we can go to work on getting the product out quicker and faster. We also look for potential "show stoppers"—problems that might affect the launch—and we work on how we might avoid these problems in the actual plan itself.

We were asked to work on a project with a consumer products company that introduces more than 400 new products per year. The project was to figure out how to speed up the process, from production to delivery. At the time we began, the company's planning process was in five-year periods. Our challenge was to answer the question: "What would it mean to the budget and bottom line if the five-year cycle could be reduced?"

Our findings were staggering. We discovered if we could ac-complish this goal, it would mean an enormous increase to the bottom line. The task was then to figure out the *how*.

So we went to work with a selected team to develop a plan to accomplish the goal of reducing the cycle. We facilitated the use of our system by taking them through each of the MICORBS phases to develop the plan and look for breakthroughs. We laid out on Displayed Thinking boards, a walk-through, a step-by step account of this five-year process. We then went back to begin the development process. We color-coded the actions that were repeated many times. One important discovery was that the majority of the action items were dealing with communications.

A meeting for approval to proceed was next, then communications to the one who missed the meeting, presentations to the others for communications and on and on. We then led the team through an idea development session to develop new, effective strategies for communicating and shrinking the time frame. Planning carefully before executing, including planning the rollout, often leads to beating the competition to the marketplace in addition to obtaining increased revenues.

Save it!

We recommend saving your rollout plans for future reference. This is a great example of using the retrieval format in the MICORBS process. Saving the plans enables you to check past launches, evaluate how you did it, then create a plan on how you can improve the next launch.

For example, we worked with a company facilitating a new sales representative training program in which we took the project through every phase of the MICORBS planning and development process. We developed a detailed rollout plan consisting of many weeks of pre-delivery work along with details, hour by hour, included in a comprehensive training course.

The project was launched successfully! The team kept the Displayed Thinking project boards as they continued to run the course by making notes on areas they could improve upon. Being able to retrieve the boards made the process of raising the bar easy.

Test the plan

This is often the forgotten step. Select a time to run a test pilot. Try the plan out. Test it and fix it, then let it roll!

In the case of Brinker International, the themed restaurant chain, we actually created a mock restaurant in a hotel ballroom and conducted a walk-through to see if any major (or minor) parts were missing so that the rollout would be seamless. Restaurants often try out new products on their senior management and assorted relatives coming for the weekend. These dry runs help prevent debacles at launch time.

Be ahead of schedule and under budget

This is opposite of what most people do on a project. We often use multiple Displayed Thinking boards to detail the issues and then tackle the solutions that pertain to the question, "How do you get a product to the consumer on time and under budget?"

We have found an important incentive for asking teams to launch the project on time and come in under budget. This is to give them a *big* reward if they do it. We don't mean the usual reward—"If you accomplish this task, you get to keep your job". We mean really big incentives that spice up the project. Create some excitement! Go beyond passing out canned hams and frozen turkeys.

Visualize, symbolize, and spiritualize

Mike was involved at Disney with the rollout of the Orlando project, Walt Disney World. There were several major components to that rollout.

One of the first phases of the rollout was to set up a top-flight training program for the preview center. Located on Lake Buena Vista, the preview center was opened to let people see what was being planned and to get them excited about the amusement complex. In the preview center, they could literally see and experience the vision. The symbol used was the majestic castle that conveyed the vision simply. Parties, celebrations, and briefings in the preview center created the continued excitement leading up to the grand opening—the launch.

A party was held for all the employees and their families. Thousands of people gathered around the castle to hear the vision, share the dream, and understand the plan. Story boards were everywhere to illustrate this new amusement park. Balloons were used to outline the buildings that were going to be erected. It was a spectacular event. Then, Disney opened the park two weeks early for the employees and their families to test the project before the launch.

The employees were offered an opportunity to earn a bonus to get the project launched on time and within budget. But the preview center and the event helped the employees to visualize, symbolize, and spiritualize the mission, which motivated them to make sure that the goals were met—with pride and satisfaction to be part of a great dream.

Exigency planning

No matter how well you plan your rollout and implementation, sometimes some things just don't work out. So what do you do? What if something doesn't get to you on time? What if you encounter a catastrophe? What is your back-up plan? What is your Plan "B"? These are critical questions.

Therefore, part of implementation and roll out should include an exigency plan for the *what-ifs*—what to do in case of an emergency. Try to identify plans that could go wrong and decide what to do. This planning will force you to resolve those issues ahead so they do not become showstoppers that make you go over budget and miss your deadlines.

Not long ago, we were working on a construction project with a company when we realized our initial plan to accomplish this difficult task would cause major traffic jams if it were executed during the daytime. We changed our timing to do this work in the late evening until early morning, thus completing it before the rush hour. We planned for the what ifs. For example, what if our construction crews burned out at this intense speed and continuous nonstop work schedule? What if equipment broke down? Our plan was to have tents set up for the crews to rest while the other crews worked along with back-up equipment on hand. Don't forget the "what if's" in your planning process. Have another one ready to go if your first one doesn't succeed.

Uncover roadblocks

When you see projects that are not coming in on schedule, projects that are not happening on time, a roadblock removal crew should be commissioned to act as your troubleshooters. This crew will uncover the roadblocks and do something about them! A good roadblock removal crew can save millions of dollars on a big project. They also boost the morale of hard-working line crews who can become frustrated at obstacles and barriers that slow them down on the job.

The chairman of one leading Fortune 500 company was trying to figure out how to break through the bureaucracy in his own company in order to make projects come in on time and under budget. One of his project teams came up with a unique solution. They asked him for a "Chairman's Corporate Bypass Card." They explained, "It gives us the right to present this card whenever we run into roadblocks for corporate 'BS' that causes whatever the policy is to be lifted or bypassed by order of the chairman." He liked the idea and gave each of them a pass that they could use three times. It was a refreshing solution from innovative leadership that contributed to great growth of the company.

Tar paper and concrete blocks

A humorous strategy to remove some of your roadblocks is one we refer to as the tar paper and concrete blocks maneuver. The idea came in jest, from Mike Vance, as a way to distract people who are a pain in the neck. All of us encounter these people, be it a mother-in-law, an obstinate child, or a nosy neighbor. What do you do when someone disrupts your efforts? Give them something to do—even if it's busywork, that they think is important.

Suppose, for example, that you are on deadline to remodel the entire lobby of a hotel and a team from corporate headquarters visits you while you're trying to work. What do you do to get them out of your hair? Get them "stuck" on something else. Have them put up tar paper on a ceiling. They'll feel productive and believe they made a great contribution—and they'll be out of your hair! It was funny to see many people doing such a useless project. If they finish with the tar paper project, ask them to move a load of concrete blocks from the front of the building to the back. (The army's been doing this for years!)

Between the tar paper, the concrete blocks, and any other "assignments" you might throw in, you can handle the people who are often roadblocks. Remember—a sense of humor is an important asset in leading the troops.

Managing your current assets

Who's covering home plate as you go for the home run?

As you begin to raise the bar in your company, how do you maintain the current business? It is imperative to make sure that in your rollout and implementation plan you identify who will be covering third base and home plate as you are hitting a home run.

This is important and needs to be thought out carefully. Do your people have the training and the proper resources? Many organizations work to raise the bar and implement a good idea only to find out they have not maintained the cash cow that keeps the company going. Raising the bar can sometimes be risky, and you may want to maintain what historically has proven to be good about something you've done in the past.

To avoid any problems, make sure you plan out the implementation, the rollout, and who will cover home plate as you go for the win. This is often referred to as "training to the next level."

The great debate

Here's where the fun begins! You have a limited budget to apply towards growth and development. Where do you place your bets? Should it be on the sacred cows adding more money to new product line extensions (which will help you raise the bar)? Or should you place some of your money on new breakthrough products that will take your business to the next level (also helping you raise the bar)? Don't ask us for the answer. Each situation is unique. Through fair debate, the right answer and pathway should prevail.

Create oil wells that can be pumped

We recommend you always have projects in the pipeline so that you keep raising the bar! Create oil wells that can be pumped when you have a need to raise the bar and fill the tank. A classic example is found within motion picture studios. They strategize a re-release program for movies and/or bring them out in a new, improved format. Think about how many times the motion picture *The Wizard of Oz* has been re-released. The studio is pumping an existing oil well.

In developing new ideas, consider all the time and research done to achieve the breakthroughs. Or in rolling out a new product or service, record the new ways you learn to achieve success. Be sure to capture this knowledge. Examine it. Ask yourself, "What can we do with that knowledge? Can we use it again, re-package it, redeploy it into new business opportunities?"

Figure out how you can get a lot out of a little and more for less. One example: A manufacturing company can analysis its equipment downtime and develop ways for better utilization. The company can get more out of what it currently has without spending more money.

Another excellent example: Disneyland began the famous "Grad Nights" at the theme park, which utilized the downtime of midnight to 8 a.m. High school students were thrilled to have a huge amusement complex all to themselves for the night. This practice generated additional revenue at relatively low costs. Try to create oils wells in your organization that can be pumped when you need a jumpstart!

Validating and measuring results

Check your rollout to evaluate whether it meets the goals and objectives of the master plan. If it tells a contradictory story, go back and rework the plan to make sure you reach the target for raising the bar.

There are many ways to measure the results of your plan. We recommend creating a subject category called "measurements." As you are developing ideas, you want to be thinking about how to measure the results and success of your work. For example, if a goal on your master plan is to increase sales by 40 percent, then list under the measurements subject category the details of how you will validate the calculation. You can also measure results by customer surveys, focused interviews, and, of course, by revenue. This step is important, especially if there are bonuses, incentives, and big rewards tied to these results.

Failed rollouts

Failed rollouts also share common characteristics: They are not carefully planned. They are not agreed upon before going to implementation. They are not properly communicated and understood by the people who will launch the plan. Plans must be realistic to be successful.

Two examples of failed rollouts were in the automobile industry. The introductions of the Edsel and the Tucker were flawed because of company politics, pricing issues, and union problems that did not come together in the rollout planning.

If you saw the movie *Tucker*, you witnessed a beautiful, cool car. But the strategies to get the car to market did not work. The Edsel had so many features on it, the car actually was too advanced for its time. Again, here are examples of unsuccessful rollouts and implementation due to poor planning. They failed because they didn't anticipate potential problems in the planning phase.

And, yes, Disney had its share of unsuccessful rollouts, too. Disneyland had to be opened quickly because Walt was running out of money. As a result, not all of the rest rooms were finished and not all of the drinking fountains were installed. People criticized these failures, and believed it was intentional not to have a drinking fountain so that more drinks would be sold. Lack of good planning and poor rollouts can lead to disastrous implementation or in some cases, no implementation at all.

Principles for raising the bar: Strategy #6

✓ Develop a rollout plan before your launch.
✓ Don't be planning your rollout while you are launching.
✓ Make sure your plan is doable and agreed upon.
✓ Have a person or people in charge of implementing.
✓ Have another plan in the pipeline ready to go.
✓ Maintain current assets as you roll out the new plans.
✓ Enhance the culture to support the new standards.

Personal applications

Countdowns

"Five, Four, Three, Two, One—Happy New Year!!"

The champagne corks pop, the noisemakers rattle, the confetti flies, and "Auld Lang Syne" is sung. Big kisses are planted on your loved ones *and* on others you don't know. What the heck. It's a celebration. Notice it all happened at the scream of *"Happy New Year."* It was planned to happen right at that moment, not 20 minutes later. Although the party can continue on for hours, it is often hard to explain the kisses that continue after the countdown.

Have you ever been to a dinner party when the main course of the meal is not served on time? Or a Fourth of July celebration when the fireworks fizzle? You're expecting a big bang—and instead you get a bust.

Plan the event and plan the rollout. You don't want to wait until the *next* year to do the celebrating. A successful rollout, whether it be for business or personal events, requires a properly timed sequence of events to get the biggest bang out of what it is you are doing.

❑ STRATEGY #8: Keep the Creative Spirit Alive and Growing

"Cultures are created and cultivated throughout history by path-finders who keep the creative spirit alive and growing—they alone raise the bar of human progress." –Diane and Mike

Passion and performance

Mike looked out of his office window at Disney Studios and observed the flag being lowered to half-mast at St. Joseph Hospital which was located across the street from the studio. He was wondering why it was being lowered when his telephone rang. He picked up the receiver.

The voice on the phone said, "Walt Disney died this morning!"

Mike's emotions overcame him as he contemplated the vast implications of what this news meant. The question of how to keep Walt's creative spirit alive and growing flashed through his mind. It would prove to be the biggest challenge in the history of the Disney organization; failure could mean a broken dream of major proportions. The challenge would be to keep his spirit and dream alive while moving forward. Fortunately, he left behind a rich legacy of knowing how to get things done, knowing how to stimulate people's passion, and knowing how to develop innovative ideas. He stood as a heroic figure to millions of people around the world. He was always raising the bar! Now, the memory of him would cause us to want to raise the bar even higher.

The contrast between Walt dying and other CEOs dying was dramatic, because Walt was loved and everyone was deeply sadden to learn of his death. When some CEOs die, people usually respond by saying "It's a shame that our CEO died, but we could always do better." In this case, his disciples were motivated to fulfill his dream, to complete the project, and to build the greatest destination resort in history. Feelings ran deep around the entire world.

The continuing challenge would be to keep his creative spirit alive. We all have heard it said many times. That seminar was great, but how can we keep our people from going right back to their same old ways on Monday? Better yet, how do we insure that they will utilize what they learned? We needed to keep Walt's passion alive. We needed to make sure we would continue to use the tools and techniques Walt had taught us. In studying all of his concepts and ideas we knew we needed to capture them in a continuing program for education and training. In order to capture and bring his methods together we followed this important strategy and the formula for success.

The strategy in raising the bar

The eighth strategy is the most strategic because it is where we find the inspiration, passion, and vision to keep us going using examples of others who have raised the bar before us. Today heroes have all but been forgotten—but their importance remains a necessity for a culture to remain viable.

It is crucial to select your personal and corporate heroes because it is here that you will discover the pathfinders who are your champions and models. We have listed a few historical pathfinders for you to consider. We recommend selecting several of them for study and research. Place books, films, and materials on them in your Team Center or Kitchens for the Mind.

We have included several vignettes on heroes that have motivated us and served as our pathfinders. We recommend that you too choose your personal heroes and learn as much from them as possible. A checkbook full of money is assuring but a checkbook full of people who can lead the way is dynamite!

Part of a good corporate heroes program is to invite guest speakers and lecturers in on a regular basis to provide knowledge and inspiration to the staff. (We know of a few we can recommend!) The Disney Company has done this for years in order to learn about the guest's leadership skills, which accounts for their strong esprit de corps among people.

Formula for success

$$\frac{I^{3+}\ P^3 = C^3}{V + M}$$

You will recall in Strategy #2 we talked about the Formula for success, which is shown above. It pointed out that throughout our work with companies, we have found that in order to have an organization that is continuously innovating and creating, you have to have people who are committed and collaborative. This sounds smart, but *how* do you actually do it? There needs to be an environment for discovery. However, a fancy environment without a creative process produces few results. You need a method to effectively stimulate creative thinking and then capture it, develop it, and get it implemented. More importantly, we need people who are using a method for keeping people informed, and keeping them inspired. The inspiration is usually the greatest challenge for many organizations. We have found very few inspiring leaders. We want leaders to have a passion, a cause, and a credo that they live by. We need a cause that will excite the teams, ignite them to rally around by raising the bar!

Leaders or pathfinders establish a vision of where you wish to raise the bar. They visualize the dream, create the spirit, and the excitement to go for it. We often find that using the technique of giving a theme to a project will give it *life* and personality. This works because most projects have no gusto, they are lifeless and usually so are the ideas they are generating. Your teams should have the tools, techniques and environments in place and ready to roll. These are the methods that will help you achieve the vision. Leaders also establish participation time with their teams. This is often accomplished in the form of briefings. Learn to bond by having powwows throughout the life of the project, giving encouragement to the teams. Celebrate achievement as much as you can because it keeps the spirit and motivation on a high plain.

How to light up the way

There's a wonderfully poignant story about a man who lived in Geneva, Switzerland, in a village called Coe. In Coe, you could look across Lake Geneva and see the French Alps' beautiful steep slopes. This man lived in a lovely community with two lovely twin daughters. Their beauty was talked about all over Switzerland more than the Alps!

One day, in a very tragic accident, the twins drowned in Lake Geneva. Their father was so distraught, so hurt and heartsick, that he decided to take all of his money and build a chapel in remembrance of his daughters, to keep their beauty and memory alive.

But when he designed it, he did something rather unusual. When he built the chapel, he purposely did so with electricity eliminated. In fact, he asked that people never install lights. Instead, he wished that each person would use a lantern when they visited the chapel. To encourage this, he inserted little pegs around the periphery of the sanctuary. The people who went to evening worship walked along the path with their lanterns to shine their way. Then, they would carry their lanterns into the chapel and place each one on a peg. When they were all inside, it lit the sanctuary. Worship service was always a very touching scene.

When asked why he insisted upon the lanterns, he explained that the purpose for building the chapel was to encourage others to bring their own light into others' lives. His daughters were his own lanterns, who brought much light into his life.

This simple lesson, as shown by the chapel, shows us the power of pathfinders and pioneers, champions and models: All of them bring their own light to life. They all light the way for the rest of us.

Bumblebee Management

Leaders who spread the praise and suggestions like bees spreading pollen on the flowers practice what we call Bumblebee Management. (See our *Think Out of the Box* book for more details on this concept.) Walt Disney was once asked by Hayley Mills, a British teenage actress shooting a film at the Disney studio, what he did around the studio. She asked if he ran a camera. He replied that he didn't. She asked if he drew animated figures. He told her he once did, but had since hired much more talented artists to do that. As the conversation went on, the actress was increasingly curious about whether Walt actually did any work.

Walt finally said to her, "I'm like a bumblebee. I go from project to project carrying ideas." Walt constantly dropped in on teams to check on their progress. He constantly challenged and encouraged them to take a simple idea and push it to its highest level. He helped people to be more creative.

Spread the spirit, continue to raise the bar

To let the spirit spread, set up more teams and give them the tools, techniques, and environments to accomplish their tasks. Select a bigger vision and set the bar higher. Share with them the vision, create the spirit, and let them go! Walt Disney did this by always having a new vision and project out in front to excite all the members of his teams. One project would be ready to launch while another was in waiting.

One way to accomplish this spreading of the spirit is for the leader to have an example of a success to share with the team. What prototype examples can you use to illustrate how to use the tools and techniques? What stories will show how to apply key concepts to current projects or problems with the goal of achieving another breakthrough success? Consequently, people are engaged in the process until the project has been implemented and completed. Thus, one great success will often lead to another great success story, which causes proliferation. Big successes spread like wildfires throughout organizations, causing everyone to want to be on the bandwagon. There is no substitute for a great cause that has inflamed passion.

Each success presents a greater challenge

Most people make the mistake by thinking they can raise the bar quicker and faster than their first time around. This may hold true for some. We have found that each time you try to come up with a greater solution, it gets harder and harder, because each time you have raised the bar by setting the standards even higher. This is an example of where we need to double or maybe triple our efforts by bringing in more resources and techniques. It often requires that we not only go the extra mile, but that we go the extra 10 miles.

Solutions for missions impossible

There are countless examples of people doing the impossible. We all remember when the earthquake in California left many highways and bridges destroyed. Normally it would take years to fix these. However, under challenging conditions, they rebuilt many of the bridges and roads in a matter of months. Whatever it is, it can be done. Most teams can accomplish extraordinary goals when given the right resources, leadership, and incentives. This is the "exigency planning" method we talked about in Strategy #7. Plan for the "what-ifs." Plan your project using this method, which will *push the limits* of your thinking. Ask the "what-ifs" over and over again. "What if we *had* to accomplish this goal by a certain date, how would we do it?" This is where breaking out of the box (Strategy #5) comes in to play. Most people don't work on accomplishing their impossible missions. Make it your most important workout for developing creative solutions. Conduct a charrette and stay on the project until you come up with a solution.

People who keep the creative spirit alive

You need to facilitate the development and implementation of projects, while keeping the energy and spirit high. You need to continue until the new ways and communication habits become part of the culture. You need to act as a coach to your team. We want to take this opportunity once again to recommend that you start a program for cultivating corporate cultures and selecting and developing pathfinders. No other program will be more important to maintaining esprit de corps or more responsible for breakthrough success. This program is the key for opening the door for your future to be greater than the past by providing a specific pathway for continuing to raise the bar. Let us show you how to do this.

Remember the pathfinders!

As you've learned, a pathfinder is a person with a vision who will get you to where you want to go. Pathfinders lead the way with a vision, often facing danger and resistance. Pathfinders know when to regroup their efforts and forge through to victory.

There are three major types of pathfinders people look up to, admire, and emulate:

> ➤ **The Champions:** They actively take up the cause, carrying its flags, and fight to the end.
> ➤ **The Heroes:** They are recognized and honored for being pathfinders.
> ➤ **The Models:** They exemplify the way and the cause, while inspiring and training others to follow.

There are a few pathfinders who display all three types of these characteristics in their personality profile, but they are rare. What do these pathfinders do and what can we expect of them?

They free the slaves.	They rescue drowning children.
They break new trails.	They refuse to quit.
They defend the oppressed.	They forge the stream.
They fall on grenades.	They go against the mob.
They aid the helpless.	They give to the poor.
They invent solutions.	They fulfill needs.
They sell their ideas.	They implement solutions.

There is, of course, an endless list of historical pathfinders around whom legends grow to inspire us to raise the bar and lift humanity to ever-higher standards and ambitions. Some of their names include:

Jesus Christ, Mohammed, Buddha, Confucius, St. Paul, Isaac Newton, Albert Einstein, Louis Pasteur, Galileo Galilei, Aristotle, Moses, Charles Darwin, Euclid, Martin Luther, Nicholas Copernicus, George Washington, Michael Faraday, William Shakespeare, Alexander Graham Bell, Thomas Jefferson, Johann Sebastian Bach, Alexander Fleming, Simón Bolívar, John Locke, Enrico Fermi, Thomas Malthus, and Voltaire, just to name a few.

Add your names to our list. Our legacy from the past is rich and illustrious, giving us insights for excellence in human conduct. We would like to present for you vignettes from our list of personal pathfinders who are champions, heroes, and models.

Pathfinders' performance

At the Creative Thinking Association's annual celebration, people who have broken out of the box by making substantial contributions to society as pathfinders are given the opportunity to speak about how they did it when they are accepting our award for creativity. Mike Markkula, co-founder of Apple Computer, said during a speech, "In order to get ahead and make the breakthroughs, you have to redouble your efforts!"

For example, we know in exercise that to burn fat and calories we have to go the extra mile, as hard as it is to do. You have to go the extra twenty minutes when doing a cardiovascular workout. You just can't stop short of the goal and expect to get big results. This simple analogy holds true also in creative thinking and raising the bar.

Most of us don't put out 100 percent in the first go around of a project, let alone do it again and again. Similarly, people make a telephone call to get a sale or come to closure on something, and then simply leave a message and forget about it. Instead, redouble your efforts again. You'll hear people say, "But, I did." Yet when you ask them what they did, their response is often, "Well, I called and left another message." That's not enough! Redouble your efforts by trying other approaches until you succeed!

In pursing a romantic relationship, most people just refuse to give up or be turned away. If you're having a hot relationship with a person and something goes wrong, you don't just throw in the towel. Instead, you redouble your efforts to try and make it work. You send flowers. If you notice this doesn't work and you're not getting anywhere, then you redouble your efforts and send two flower arrangements. Maybe you throw in a box of candy. Perhaps some diamonds—they always tend to get people's attention! We often redouble our efforts when we're pursing a person, but give up too quickly when it's time to salvage an existing relationship.

The iconoclast

Steve Jobs is a fantastic pathfinder and champion in every way, according to Mike. He is a model for redoubling his efforts in the face of adversity. Mike has known Steve since he started Apple Computer and has spent hours with him talking philosophy and dreaming about the future. Steve has been an inspiration for what he was able to accomplish, for constantly redoubling his efforts. He's not a quitter, a compromiser, or a person who goes along to appease someone. He continues to think out of the box no matter what happens to him.

Some people only know one side of Steve's personality and have been extremely critical of him. He is truly a remarkable person. Before he was twenty, he set out to create one of the most extraordinary companies in the world.

Along the way, he got knocked down, dragged through the ditch, and beaten up regularly. Mike was there with him through much of it in the early days. When he was squashed, guess what he did? He got back up, redoubled his efforts and went right on to continue building a magnificent company.

Mike talked with Steve's team when he started NeXt, where once again he was knocked down. Once again, he got right back up and redoubled his efforts. Out of his experiences, yet another dream developed of wanting to do the type of great things that

Walt Disney pioneered in animation. The result? He founded a company most people are familiar with if you've seen the movies *Toy Story* and *A Bug's Life*. *Toy Story*, which won an academy award, was the first picture out of the new company called Pixar, Steve Jobs's studio. What a champion! Then, he went back to help Apple Computer to redouble their efforts again.

During a recent dinner at Steve's house, he spoke with Mike, Vanessa, and John Vance for several hours about Walt Disney and what he was really like as a man. Steve said that he wanted to be like Walt in the sense that he would like to be a pioneer in the field of animation like Walt had done. No doubt that Steve, with the Pixar staff, will do just that. Mike had a discussion with the Pixar team in Berkeley not long ago and found that the spirit was there to accomplish greatness all over again. Never count Steve Jobs out. Steve will no doubt have setbacks in the future because he's pioneering, rather than doing the same old tired things. He's blazing new trails. And after all, he is a champion and model for not only redoubling his efforts, but also for creating a dream, having a vision, and turning the dream and the vision into reality.

Raising the bar in your company's culture

You hear the term "company culture" being used freely all of the time. What do people really mean when they use this term? A company culture is a combination of many factors: special traditions, rituals, symbols, language, unique ways to celebrate victories, work habits, and workspaces. In essence, it is the climate or environment that makes your organization distinctly unique.

Survival in today's world of business depends on maintaining company cultures that stimulate people and encourage them to continuously raise the bar and go the extra mile. When raising the bar in an organization, you must analyze the culture of the organization to see if it will support the new venture. Often, when raising the bar, you must enhance and cultivate the corporate culture. To create breakthrough solutions it often require new ways of thinking and working together. You want to keep these breakthrough solutions coming. You want the bar chart to keep going up and not look like the stock market crash of October 1929. This usually requires new work habits and environments that stimulate innovative thinking and exceptional planning for implementation.

There are a few steps that you can take to develop a culture for individuals as well as your organization. First, remember that symbols are your ideas made visible. These symbols that you want to make visible in developing a culture are those that have value, and are what you consider to be important. Therefore, the first action that you want to take is to have what we call "valuing sessions." These sessions help you to identify the values that are going to drive your organization and support how you can develop them into a symbol.

We think the Disney organization is one of the greatest examples in the world. Disney holds the laughter of children, educational experiences, and fun for all ages as the goals of their company. And their appropriate symbol? The ubiquitous Mickey Mouse.

AT&T used the horse carousel that Walt Disney designed for Disneyland as a symbol for one of their divisions. Walt Disney saw a carousel where all the horse didn't jump and said, "Let's build a place where all the horses jump." AT&T's translation of the carousel, which they created into a pin, was that they wanted all of the "horses to jump" as a symbol, to go the extra mile, and to give people extra service.

Describe your corporate culture

If someone were to walk up to you right now and ask you to "describe your corporate culture," what would you say? Could you do it? What does it look like? Be realistic. Be honest. If it's bad, make sure to say so. Good corporate cultures don't just happen, you have to plan them. You can't just order them and have them installed on Monday. You need to incorporate techniques, methods, and habits into your environment to continue to grow your culture. And you need a plan of action that will enhance the growth of your company and not be diluted by the growth. When companies merge or get acquired, a plan should be developed that takes the best of both organizations and creates a new and better culture.

How to perpetuate the cultural change

Ask yourself, "Am I thinking or am I just reacting?" Create a culture of continuous innovation and creativity. Make it part of your daily work habit and routine. Have a process to jump-start and improve the quality of your thinking.

---

1. Reason for cultural enhancement/change.

Make sure people know why the change is needed.

Explain the reason behind the change.

Relate cause to effect.

2. Inspiration through facilitation (top-down).

Inspire the people with whom you want to make the change.

Vision/dream, goal/objective.

Where are we going? Create blue prints for change.

Present concepts and examples.

3. Team involvement (bottom-up).

How to get there.

Team Centers, Environments for Discovery, briefings, and so forth.

Pathfinder programs.

4. Implementation crew.

Assemble roadblock removal crews.

Remove obstacles that block the roll-outs.

Why do people resist?

1. Disagree with the vision.

2. Fear results of change.

3. Vision not clear.

4. See new roadblocks.

5. Inexperienced.

As you strive to raise the bar, keep in mind that the reason rollouts and launches fail is that they don't take into consideration the four major ways to perpetuate cultural growth. Every time you raise the bar, you change the culture just a little bit. You need to make sure you enhance the culture to support the higher standards or the bar may come tumbling down! When Disney added Disneyland to his organization, he added a whole new business. The bar was raised. When he created his resort in Orlando, the bar was raised again. The Disney culture supported new work habits and implemented innovative plans.

The first method for perpetuating cultural growth is to identify the reasons for cultural enhancement. Make sure people know why the change is needed. Determine how you will share this with your people. Will it be with an advanced event, or similar to a preview center? What are your expectations? However you decide this communication will take place, it should become an element of your master plan.

Next, you must inspire through skilled facilitation. How can you inspire people below us on the corporate ladder, and how do you inspire people to want to participate in the change? Recall that inspiration is not just charisma, but that inspiration comes from people who exemplify the possibilities of what it is you want to achieve. The key to this is to reflect the vision, share the goals and the dreams of the company, and hold them up as good examples. It isn't the same to have someone tell you that you should take piano lessons when they have never sat down in front of a piano themselves. It doesn't work.

The third method we've outlined is team involvement. To involve your team and get them onboard your plan, we recommend using Displayed Thinking in a Team Center, as it gets people involved just by walking into the room. They see exactly what it is that's going on and then become eager to participate. Displayed Thinking offers a framework to bring order out of chaos and becomes an environment for discovery. Address the issues. Get the team involved!

The implementation crew is the final method to initiate cultural change, and it is extremely necessary. When you change a corporate culture and raise your bar, you'll get people that will resist. Certain people will complain even though most people want a new experience and look forward to new initiatives that will cause them to grow and prosper. But the principal reason people resist is that they disagree with the vision. If this occurs, it is the kind of a problem you have to "work out."

The technique of the workout is very useful. You get all of your team in a room and stay there until you come to closure on the issues you're going to resolve and put them into deliverables and launch. If people fear the results of change, one of the actions that your implementation crew should do is to alleviate the fears of people by showing them realistically the positive points that the change can bring about. If there are negatives, don't try to cover them up. Discuss them with your team and try to shed light on how they can be turned into positives. (Be sure to listen to our "Cultivating Company Cultures" audio program for additional information and insight.)

New traditions

Keeping the creative spirit alive and growing requires an organization to establish new traditions. Traditions can be any area of corporate endeavor: new work habits, new initiatives, new language, new celebrations, new incentives, new environments, and so forth.

When raising the bar, your corporate culture needs to support the pathway that lead to the success, so you can continue the process and raise the bar higher!

What are some traditions and rituals today in your organization and in your personal life? Write them down! Then list what may be some new ones you would like to add and reinforce the creative spirit that was awakened.

Three-job concept

An example of a new tradition is the use of the three-job concept. The program consists of:

1. Performing the job that you were hired to do.
2. Sharing your knowledge and insights. Always be working on or participating on a project. Most everyone has ideas to contribute. Organizations usually have a wealth of knowledge in their employees but rarely let them participate or ask them for their input on projects or problems. So often it is because they don't have a method or system that makes this easy. The MICORBS Process and the Displayed Thinking System enables this to happen at a glance, reducing time and saving money.
3. Always have each person in some sort of learning situation. Always be training or mentoring to the next level so that as you raise the bar, your people are right there with new skills to help implement solutions.

When we talk about this concept, we often hear people say, "Well, we are too busy. We don't have time for that stuff." Walt Disney believed that the most creative organizations were the ones that were the most organized. Why? Because being organized allowed them time to do creative thinking and take up some of these new initiatives.

Mahatma Ghandhi's wisdom

Mahatma Ghandhi raised the bar for social justice higher and higher during his lifetime. He kept the creative spirit alive and growing in the hearts of millions of followers. He was a blessing to humanity. His grandson Arun Ghandhi wrote:

"In October 1947, when I went to say my final farewell to my grandfather, Mahatma Ghandhi, so that I could accompany my parents to South Africa, Grandfather slipped a paper in my hand and said, 'Keep this as a Talisman. What I have written here are the Seven Blunders that the human society commits, which cause all violence. Work to change this.'"

We recommend you consider these in enhancing the culture of your organization so that they don't become blunders in your organization. Arun Ghandhi added the eighth blunder:

Blunders of the World:

1. Wealth without work.
2. Pleasure without conscience.
3. Knowledge without character.
4. Commerce without morality.
5. Science without humanity.
6. Worship without sacrifice.
7. Politics without principles.
8. Rights without responsibilities.

Principles for raising the bar: Strategy #8

✓ Spread the word with examples of successes for others to emulate.

✓ Establish projects that will set the bar higher.

✓ Identify pathfinders and have pathfinder development plans and programs in the organization.

✓ Cultivate your company culture to support raising the bar.

✓ Develop new traditions that support the new culture and keep the creative spirit alive and growing.

✓ Avoid blunders in your organization.

✓ Make sure you have completed all eight strategies for raising the bar.

✓ Set the bar again higher than before!

✓ Select heroes, champions, and models to learn from.

✓ Don't believe that raising the bar will be incredibly easy.

✓ Have a formula and plan on how you will raise the bar.

✓ Work on "Missions Impossible" to achieve Breakthrough Solutions.

✓ Select people who know how to inspire others.

✓ Have a well thought out plan on how to keep the creative spirit alive and growing.

Personal applications

The Senator

An inspiring example of a person who got knocked down, but got back up is Senator Max Cleland. We had the good fortune to meet and dine with this heroic figure, who has become a role model and champion. He understood raising the bar to new heights, despite a life threatening adversity.

Max Cleland was born in Atlanta, Georgia, in 1942 and grew up in Lithuania. He went to school at Stetson University and went on to receive his master's degree in American History at Emory University. In 1967, he stuck his neck out by volunteering for combat duty in Vietnam. He was promoted to the rank of captain in the U.S. Army before he was seriously wounded in a fierce grenade explosion. He was awarded the Silver Star for gallantry in action for his service.

Back from the war, Cleland was elected to the Georgia State Senate in 1970 at the age of 28. As the youngest member of the state senate and the only Vietnam veteran, he drafted the state law that made public facilities accessible to the elderly and the handicapped. In 1977, President Jimmy Carter appointed him to head the U.S. Veterans Administration. This was unprecedented, as he became the youngest administrator ever, as well as the first veteran of Vietnam to head the agency.

He published *Strong at the Broken Places* in 1980, his autobiography about his war experiences. Georgia voters went on to elect Max Cleland secretary of state in 1982. In that position, he fought for tougher campaign finance laws, cracked down on securities and telemarketing fraud, and implemented the "National Voter Registration Act," which added more than one million new Georgia voters to the rolls. He created a one-stop shop for small business owners and entrepreneurs, and won a national award from the U.S. Small Business Administration.

Cleland was elected to replace Sam Nunn in the United States Senate by the Georgia voters in 1996. He became a member of the Senate Armed Services Committee, and currently serves as the ranking Democrat on it. He is leading efforts in the Personnel

Subcommittee to make improvements in military health care for members of the Armed Forces, their families, and retirees.

He was named by *Time* magazine on a list of rising Democrats in 1996. He has been called "America's most extraordinary politician" by *The London Times*. David Brodow of *The Washington Post* has written that Cleland is "the genuine article." "He is everywhere; a living, breathing testament to the power of the human spirit."

What we haven't told you is that Senator Max Cleland is handicapped. A war accident left him with two amputated legs and only half of one arm. Yet this amazing man redoubled his efforts, raised the bar to new heights, and became a true champion and model for us all.

However, if you ever meet Senator Cleland, you'll realize that he isn't handicapped. Starting in grade school, like many American children, he stood each morning to recite these famous words: "I pledge allegiance to the flag of the United States of America, and to the republic for which it stands, one nation, under God, indivisible, with liberty and justice for all."

We too have created a pledge that we dedicated to Senator Max Cleland. The pledge of the champion was created to inspire and proclaim oneself to think out of the box and stand out from the crowd.

"I pledge allegiance to myself, and to what I can become, one person among the many, below no one, unique, with the possibilities and potential I have, to reach, to dream, to raise the bar."

The Cowboy

Mike tells us about a childhood hero of his—Gene Autry:

"My grandfather and father owned a grocery store in downtown Greenville, Ohio, home of the famed sharpshooter, Annie Oakley, and popular radio commentator Lowell Thomas. I started working around the store when I was five years old, just as soon as I was old enough to be of value. I especially remember an incident that took place early one Saturday morning when I was in the fifth grade.

"There were small streets in the back of the store called alleys in the 1930s. In the alley directly behind the grocery store, there was a large living trailer parked next to the building and beside it was a horse van pulled by a pick-up truck. There was a man sleeping behind the driver's seat in the truck. Instantly, I recognized him as Gene Autry, the famous singing cowboy. I had seen him perform the night before on the stage of the State Theater.

"I approached the open window with some trepidation. Mr. Autry spoke to me, 'Good morning young fellow. Do you have any water around here?' I said that we did have water in the store. He handed me a jug, which I took into the store and filled it with water from the sink in the back room. I ran out and gave him the jug through the open window. He said, 'Thank you young fellow. Let me know if I can ever return the favor.'

"I was thrilled to meet Gene Autry, but never did it occur to me that years later I would ask him to return the favor. But that is exactly what happened nearly 30 years later in Los Angeles, California. Gene Autry would return the favor.

"I was producing and hosting the television show *Men at the Top* on KNBC television in Los Angeles. We were seeking a permanent station and sponsor to negotiate a one-year contract. Gene Autry owned the popular television station KTLA 5 in the Los Angeles market and would be an ideal station for airing my show. Luck was with me, and I managed to get an appointment to see Mr. Autry.

"On the appointed day, I walked into his office at Golden West Broadcasting with the same trepidation that I had felt as a little boy in Greenville. He was very gracious and friendly as we met each other in the doorway of his office.

"'How can I help you young man?' he asked.

"'I have a television show that I want to sell you, Mr. Autry,' I replied.

"'You'll have to talk with my program director, Loring Dueseau, about that,' he said.

"'I'll do that Mr. Autry if you can get me in to see him. But I wanted to tell you that we have met before in Greenville, Ohio, when I was a little boy. I gave you a jug of water from our grocery store on Saturday morning and you said to let you know if you could ever return the favor.'

"'Yes, I remember you and the water,' he laughed. 'It was the Broadway Grocery. Your grandfather let me park my trailer and van behind his store whenever I was in town for a show. I think Loring will be glad to see you.'

"I saw Loring and my show, *Men at the Top*, began the following Saturday night on KTLA TV. Gene Autry had fulfilled a 30-year-old promise that is reflected in his Cowboy's creed throughout his life—a cowboy must never go back on his word and above all else, be a straight shooter. The hallmark of a hero was stamped across Gene Autry's life."

☐ EPILOGUE:
Being Cool, Courageous, Clever, and Competent

We have explored eight strategies that guide these entrepreneurial voyagers on their trips in discovering new worlds of enterprise. However, there remains one additional attribute that we reserved for the epilogue, because it rounds out the content of this book. Here, Mike gives an account of a recent experience that highlights the special quality of those who raise the bar:

"My airplane landed on a bone-chilling day at the Rochester, Minnesota airport. I was on my way to the famous Mayo Clinic where I was to speak to the board of governors and a group of doctors early the next morning. It had been over ten years since I spoke at the clinic. I was anxious to return because of my deep respect for the exceptional medical expertise of this pioneering institution. The Mayo Clinic typifies the spirit of pathfinding that we discussed earlier.

"As we were taxiing to the arrival gate, I glanced out of my airplane window and saw a large private jet parked in the adjacent gate. The inscription on the side of the plane caught my attention—fast.

"The inscription read, "The Royal Hashemite Kingdom of Jordan!" There was a huge crown covering the entire tail section—the king's monogram. I realized it was the private plane that was bringing King Hussein to the Mayo Clinic for cancer treatment. My respect for the clinic was further validated, considering that he flew all the way from Jordan many times to help fight his cancer...which a few days later took his life.

"Early the next morning, my work began when I spoke at 7 a.m. to a large group of doctors and hospital staff in the clinic's auditorium. Even though it was early in the morning, they were a receptive and responsive audience. Dr. John Noseworthy, chair of the Department of Neurology, consulted with me after the meeting, and was great to work with. My respect for the Mayo Clinic just continued to rise.

"I was then escorted to the executive offices by Kenneth Kurth, who helped in preparing me for my meeting with the board of governors. The chair of the Mayo Clinic Board of Governors, Dr. Hugh Smith, came in to greet me, discussing what he hoped we could achieve during my working session with his board.

"I liked Dr. Smith immediately. He is one of those rare people who reached the top of his field yet remained warm and human. Also, I was soon to discover his fabulous sense of humor when he introduced me to the board. A highly developed sense of humor is another characteristic found in those who raise the bar.

"Entering the boardroom, I was introduced informally to the members and listened to several presentations of the future of the clinic. The quality of their thinking impressed me as I listened to the logic of their planning.

"Dr. Smith then introduced me. It was terrific! He had one of those small joke boxes with a voice captured inside that shouted 'let me out of here' when you touched it. After the customary introduction, he placed the box in the center of the table...and it shouted rather loudly! Dr. Smith said, 'That's what Mike is going to do for us—get us out of the box.' It was a perfect introduction that really broke the ice for me. I didn't need a warm up and started in high gear.

"This is part of what I said:

"'Your great success at the Mayo Clinic has been your long history of staying out of the box and continually raising the bar of performance to higher and higher standards. We have been investigating and studying the qualities of those people who think out of the box at the Creative Thinking Association for over twenty years. What are these individuals like who achieve major breakthroughs in every field of endeavor? What are the personality characteristics that we observe in these pioneers of innovation, creativity, and invention?

"'You all realize these characteristics are difficult to pin down, measure, and really study objectively. There are many academics and theorists who say it really cannot be done—that we're just guessing.

"However, we have observed another very specific quality in the creators we have known or studied in the course of our work!'

"At this point, I noticed that nearly every board member had his or her pens poised and ready to write down what this quality is.

"We found that they have one major attribute in common, one defining characteristic or quality—they are cool."

Several people looked at me as if they hadn't heard what I said. When they realized that I did indeed say "cool," they all had a good laugh, kidding each other about their coolness. But, silently we all knew that people who think out of the box continually are cool!

The board was leaving for a three day planning retreat following our meeting and I suggested they might talk about some of these ideas on their retreat. Several days after their retreat, I talked with Dr. Smith on the phone. He said they had a successful planning retreat. But best of all, he said that their spirits were soaring on the way home. He told me that they were singing high school songs on the bus ride home. Of course, I said that it was "cool."

We would like you to consider your own "coolness"! We want you to experience the cool spirit, much like the Mayo Clinic Board of Governors did!

What qualities make you cool?

We know that utilizing the eight strategies to set up a Raise the Bar program in your company can set the stage for being cool in the deepest sense. Let's highlight what you have learned:

➢ Build a Strong Foundation (Strategy #1)
➢ Think Out of the Box (Strategy #2)
➢ Create a Master Plan (Strategy #3)
➢ Develop People and Pathfinders (Strategy #4)
➢ Break Out of the Box (Strategy #5)
➢ Communicate and Organize (Strategy #6)

➢ Roll Out and Implement (Strategy #7)

➢ Keep the Creative Spirit Alive and Growing (Strategy #8)

We have observed that those who raise the bar employ all eight of these strategies during their pursuits of excellence, while being cool, courageous, clever, and competent in their actions.

For example, Bruce McCaw, president of the Pac West Racing Group, recently asked Mike to give his Pac West racing team (including racers like Mark Blundell and Mauricio Gugelman) a full day Think Out of the Box Seminar. It was a bold move exposing a racing team to a seminar designed to enhance innovation, teamwork, and leadership skills. McCaw defended his decision. Bruce said, "I believe this seminar will give our people the tools to work together more successfully in the coming season. It is important for people to think in ways they haven't before."

You can see that Bruce is definitely a cool guy. The Pac West championship racing team is cool, courageous, competent and clever by adding intellect to their outstanding physical abilities.

The 4 "Cs" for raising the bar

To raise the bar to new heights, you will need to be cool, courageous, clever, and competent. What do each of these qualities involve? Read the following list and find out!

Cool is:

➢ Stimulating high spirits.

➢ Developing breakthrough ideas.

➢ Helping people become their best.

➢ Having a great sense of humor.

➢ Being passionate, warm, and human.

Courageous is:

➢ Telling the truth when it needs to be faced.

➢ Eager to seek new pathways.

➢ Selling your ideas and point of view.

➢ Not fearful of making changes when needed.

➢ Breaking new ground.

Clever is:

➤ Being sharp, brainy, alert, skillful, ingenuous, and above all, creative.

Competent is:

➤ Not sanctioning incompetence in yourself or others.
➤ Seeking out new knowledge and resources when required.
➤ Being good at what you do.
➤ Being successful.

We hope you will always strive to raise the bar higher and higher! You have no place to go but up! Learn how to keep motivation simple and effective, and never lose sight of your vision!

For further information on our various products, services, and ways to raise the bar, contact us at:

The Creative Thinking Association
16600 Sprague Road, Suite 120
Cleveland, OH 44130
Phone: (440)243-5576
Fax: (440)243-8754
E-Mail: thinkcta@aol.com
Website: http://www.creativethinkingassoc.com

□ INDEX

Index